# HAMLYN ALL COLOUR
# HERBS AND AROMATICS

# HAMLYN ALL COLOUR
# HERBS AND AROMATICS

HAMLYN

Editor  Isobel Holland
Art Editor  Susan Michniewicz
Picture Research  Caroline Hensman
Production  Nick Thompson

Illustrations by Vicky Emptage
Symbols by Coryn Dickman

First published in Great Britain in 1993
by Hamlyn an imprint of Reed Consumer Books Limited
Michelin House, 81 Fulham Road, London SW3 6RB
and Auckland, Melbourne, Singapore and Toronto

© 1993 Reed International Books Limited

A catalogue record for this book is available
from the British Library

ISBN 0 600 57643 4

Typeset in Sabon

Produced by Mandarin Offset
Printed in Hong Kong

The Publishers would like to thank the following individuals and organisations
for providing the photographs used in this book:

A-Z Botanical Collection half-title page, 68 left, 72 left, 87 right; Bernard Alfieri back cover top left, 43 right;
K & G Beckett 107 right; Boys Syndication 6, 24 right, 77 left, 80, /Jacqui Hurst front cover right,
19, 28 right, 85 right; Pat Brindley title page left, 50 left, 61 right, 77 right, 109 left, 116;
Eric Crichton back cover top right, back cover bottom left and bottom right, 18,
21 left and right, 23 right, 25 right, 28 left, 30 right, 31 right, 36 left, 38, 39, 41 right, 42 right,
43 left, 46 left, 47 left, 48 right, 50 right, 51 right, 56 left and right, 57 right, 59 left and right,
62 left and right, 69 left, 70 right, 71 right, 73 left, 74 left, 78 left, 82 left and right, 84 left,
88 right, 90 right, 95 left, 100 left, 101 left, 102 left, 105 left, 108 right, 109 right,
111 right, 113 right, 115 left, 119 left, 121 left and right, 122 right, 123 right;
Floracolour 87 left; Brian Furner 25 left, 96 left; Garden Picture Library/Derek Fell 37 left;
Derek Gould 96 right, 110 right; Andrew Lawson 51 left, 55 left, 65 right, 68 right, 73 right, 85 left, 120 right;
Tania Midgely 22 left, 46 right, 120 left; Clive Nichols 11, 12, 52, 66, 67, 93;
Photos Horticultural title page centre and right, 36 right, 40 left, 58 left, 60 right, 61 left, 69 right, 72 right, 75 right,
83 left and right, 84 right, 86 left, 91 left, 97 right, 105 right, 106 left, 115 right;
Reed International Books Ltd. 32 right, 74 right, /Michael Boys front cover left, 22 right, 26 right,
27 right, 30 left, 32 left, 37 right, 44 left, 45 right, 55 right, 63 right, 64 right, 70 left, 76 left,
100 right, 101 right, 103 left and right, 108 left, 110 left, 111 left, 118 right, 125 right, /W. F. Davidson 20 right, 26 left,
44 right, 97 left, /Jerry Harpur back cover centre, 48 left, 54 left and right, 58 right, 65 left, 71 left, 76 right,
78 right, 4 left, 95 right, 98 left, 99 left and right, 107 left, 112 left and right, 114 right, 124 left and right,
/Neil Holmes 20 left, 23 left, 24 left, 29 left, 33 right, 31 left, 34 left and right, 35 right, 123 left,
/George Wright 49 right, 64 left, 75 left, 79 right, 94 right, 104 left and right, 113 left, 114 left, 122 left, 125 left;
Harry Smith Horticultural Photographic Collection front cover centre, 27 left, 29 right, 33 left, 35 left,
40 right, 42 left, 47 right, 49 left, 57 left, 60 left, 63 left, 79 left, 86 right, 88 left, 89 left, 90 left, 91 right,
98 right, 102 right, 106 right, 118 left, 119 right; Peter Stiles 8, 13, 92; Thompson & Morgan (Ipswich) 41 left.

# CONTENTS

# IN THE AROMATIC GARDEN

'...what rarer object can there be on earth... than a beautiful and Odiferous Garden plot...'

So wrote Thomas Hill, the author of the first gardening book written in English in the seventeenth-century, and it would be difficult to contradict him over 300 years later. Enjoyable though it is, there is no doubt that gardening can be hard work, but the reward for all that planning, digging and planting makes it worthwhile – an environment created to your own specifications. Think how much more enjoyable your leisure time in the garden will be if, in addition to the colours and shapes of plants you have cultivated, you can enjoy their scent and, as a delightful bonus, the humming of bees and the colour of butterflies drawn to their aromatic flowers .

Adding scent to your garden in a systematic way, choosing plants with good scent as well as for their other characteristics, and planting in such a way as to enhance their perfume makes gardening much more satisfying, and will make your garden unforgettable.

You don't need a large garden to grow herbs and aromatic plants, you don't even need a special area for them, although that is a possibility you might want to consider. The added dimension of aroma can be introduced throughout the whole garden, simply by choosing and planning with scent in mind, and this book will show you how.

## SCENTED PLANT HISTORY

The history of herbs and aromatics must be as old as that of man. The first documented evidence we have of herbs being used for medicinal purposes dates from 2000BC in Babylon, but equally ancient are the uses of scented and aromatic plants for cooking, perfume, dyeing, disinfecting, and religious ceremonies. The Greeks and Romans added their skill to a body of ancient knowledge which spread through Europe with the Roman Empire. More than 200 different herbs were introduced by the Romans into Britain, including sage, borage, fennel, rosemary and thyme.

Once the Roman Empire fell, however, much of that skill was lost in Europe, although religious orders took over the role of cultivating herbs and aromatic plants in monastery gardens, and a native herbal folklore was developed in towns and villages.

The shift from gardening for utilitarian purposes to creating decorative gardens for pleasure can be seen as representing the moment when a civilisation becomes mature. During the Renaissance, a number of important ornamental gardens were constructed, particularly in Italy, yet the cultivation of herbs and aromatics was continuing with even greater enthusiasm with the first botanical garden being constructed in Padua in 1545. With the development of the printing press, the uses to which herbs could be put were made more widely known, in particular with the publication of two well-known English herbals, one by John Gerard and the other by Nicholas Culpeper. The range of herbs and aromatics on which these early practitioners could draw was extending rapidly, as explorers brought back plants native to newly discovered lands, to be experimented with and incorporated into the physic gardens of the time.

Of necessity, early settlers in colonized countries rapidly developed an understanding of the strange and exotic flora they encountered in their new lands, frequently helped and guided by the indigenous peoples. In return, they established plants they had brought with them from their mother countries and a rich botanical exchange was established.

With the industrial revolution, a rich legacy was lost as the rural population moved to towns, particularly in northern Europe. For some, life became easier

*To achieve such a delightful setting requires thought, planning and hard work. Based on an Italian design this garden incorporates a wisteria arch (back) and a mixture of low-growing bulbs, annuals and shrubs.*

and gardening developed into a pastime indulged in chiefly for its ornamental value. Herbs could be bought, perfumes and dyes too, and medicines were produced in factories, so who, in an industrialized society, would bother to grow them? Fortunately, the old respect for herbs and aromatics survived in rural communities around the world, and now the wheel has turned full circle. The desire to return to pre-industrial ways, with unprocessed food, organically raised vegetables, natural cosmetics and medicines reflects the anxiety of a society suddenly becoming aware of all that it has lost. By planting herbs and aromatic plants in your practical, yet ornamental garden you can have the best of both worlds, and gain a greater understanding of the many benefits that these time-honoured plants can have for you in a modern world.

# KNOW YOUR GARDEN

As with all garden projects, avoid making hasty decisions. This does not mean that you can sit back and do nothing. On the contrary, spend some time observing carefully what is already in your garden and what condition it is in, deciding what you want to keep and what you have to discard. Make a ground plan and identify areas of shade and full sun, throughout the year as the angle of the sun changes, and in all weathers – what you think of as a shady border might have plenty of sun in the morning, for example, or in late autumn when nearby trees start to loose their leaves. Be aware of the direction of the prevailing wind. All these details will affect your choice of plants.

Try to become familiar with the kind of soil in your garden. It can vary from one part of the garden to another, so test widely. There are three main things you need to know about your soil. The first is the texture of the soil, the second is the structure, and the third is the pH.

**SOIL TEXTURE** What we blithely term soil is a combination of many ingredients: water, air, organic matter and mineral particles in varying amounts. The texture of your soil can be classified according to the proportions of sand, silt and clay it contains, and there are three major categories: light, medium and heavy. Peat, being an organic rather than mineral soil, is considered separately. The lighter soils contain a high proportion of sand, the medium contain roughly the same proportion of sand as silt and clay, and heavy soils contain more clay. If you are uncertain what the texture of your soil is, you can form an idea simply by going outside and getting your hands dirty.

If you have a clay soil you are probably only too aware of the fact – it is a cold soil, slow to warm up in spring and heavy to work. A sure sign of heavy soil is that it sticks to your shoes in lumps when wet, and forms a solid mass when compacted. When moist clay is rubbed between finger and thumb, the surface becomes shiny and smooth. Drainage is often a problem with heavy soils – they waterlog in wet weather, yet they shrink and crack in the dry. The plus side for clay soils is that they tend to be rich in nutrients.

A light, sandy soil is easy to cultivate and warms up early in the growing season. It will not stick to your boots in wet conditions, and will feel gritty if rubbed between your fingers. Even if moist, it cannot easily be squeezed to form a mass that will hold together. The main disadvantages are that it is very free-draining, and dries out quickly. In addition, plant nutrients are quickly lost from light soils, washed out by the rain. Frequent watering and feeding will be necessary.

Medium soils, or loams are ideal for most purposes, as they are mid-way between the two extremes and have the advantages of both, usually without the disadvantages. They generally have a crumb-like structure which will re-emerge if you compact the soil then break it up again with your fingers. The main challenge with medium soils is to maintain their condition.

**SOIL STRUCTURE** The structure of your soil is the way the particles group together and, unlike the texture, it is something you can change by the way you cultivate and what you add. Whatever texture soil you start with, you can optimize its structure and approach the ideal open 'crumb structure' that allows movement of air, water and, therefore, roots through the soil. Equally, a good soil structure can be destroyed by compaction or excessive cultivation. If your soil structure is faulty, the time and money you devote to choosing and buying plants will all be wasted, so start with your soil – once that is right, everything else will follow.

For heavy clay soils, start by resolving not to walk on them or compact them in any way when they are wet. Cultivate in autumn, but leave in lumps so that winter frosts will play their part in breaking up the soil. Adding coarse grit, although expensive, will help to open up the structure but it is even more important to dig in as much organic matter as you can lay your hands on. Garden compost is the obvious choice, but well-rotted stable manure or leaf mould will help preserve the crumb structure you have created and introduce beneficial soil bacteria. Lime is sometimes suggested as a useful addition for clay soil and, if sprinkled on in autumn (unless you have added manure, in which case wait until early spring), in the form of hydrated lime or ground limestone it helps clay particles to bind together into crumbs. If your soil is already alkaline – something you should check with a pH test

– adding lime will just make it more so, and this will lead to nutritional deficiencies in your plants. Instead of lime, under these circumstances, use gypsum in the same way.

Peat can also be a heavy soil and slow to warm up in spring if the water content is high, but in its favour its texture is spongy and it is high in organic matter. If waterlogged, work may be needed to correct drainage. Its low pH will make adding lime a necessity to extend the range of plants you can grow, and extra fertilizers will be needed frequently .

For light soils, also add organic matter. Again, your own compost, if you can produce enough, well-rotted farmyard manure,  which is heavier than stable manure, or a green manure, but these should  be incorporated into the top layer of soil, not dug in too deeply or the benefits will be lost. The addition of bulky organic matter will help the water-holding capacity of sandy soil, and bind the particles together to form the all-important crumbs. Soil fertility will also be improved because nutrients will not leach from the soil as much as before. Try not to over- cultivate by digging or raking too much or the crumbs will break down again into light, sandy particles.

Chalky soils benefit from the same treatment. They are usually shallow, with a thin layer of topsoil over a crumbly chalk subsoil, so adding organic matter as a mulch will increase the depth of topsoil and contribute to bringing down the pH, or reducing alkalinity, which is always a problem with chalk. Fertilizer will be needed often .

For medium soils or loams, maintenance is still required to keep them in good condition. Left uncultivated, a medium soil would remain much the same, but the demands made on the soil by gardening – intensive cropping, digging and planting – gradually use up the supply of humus and nutrients in the soil. These need to be replaced by incorporating bulky organic matter, occasionally adding lime, which is gradually used up in the soil, and by selectively applying fertilizers.

**SOIL pH** Before you choose any plants, you need to know what your soil pH is – whether your soil is neutral, with a pH of around 7, alkaline, with a higher reading, or acid, with a lower reading. This information is also important when you are choosing fertilizers or soil conditioning treatments, which may have an effect on the pH themselves. You can buy a simple kit to test for this, but even without a kit there are plenty of clues about the pH of your soil from plants growing in the area. Rhododendrons, camellias, primulas and most types of heather indicate an acid soil, while clematis, lavenders and pinks prefer an alkaline, or limy soil. Acid conditions prevail in peat or sometimes sandy soils where the rainfall is heavy, alkaline soil is often associated with chalk or limestone bedrock.

The majority of plants do best at a pH of between 6.5 and 7.3, which is more or less neutral, but some, such as camellias and rhododendrons, require acid conditions and, if grown on soil with too much lime will suffer from nutritional deficiencies, weaken, and the leaves will turn yellow. Most herbs do well on a neutral to slightly alkaline soil, although roses thrive on neutral to slightly acid conditions. A very acid soil can be normalized by the addition of hydrated lime or ground limestone, but it is difficult to reduce the pH of a strongly alkaline soil. There is a list of plants suitable for alkaline soils *(see page 16)*

**SOIL NUTRIENTS** For healthy, strong growth, plants must be fed. Adding bulky organic matter can provide some nutrients, but it is difficult to tell which and how much. This is why fertilizer must be added to ensure your plants are getting the food they need. The main chemical elements that plants need, usually in quite large amounts, are nitrogen, phosphorous and potassium, usually abbreviated to N, P and K. They all have a number of important roles in plant function, but basically Nitrogen is necessary for green, leafy growth, Phosphorous is important for healthy root development and potassium increases flowering and fruiting and improves disease resistance. Although it is sometimes necessary to apply just one of these elements for a specific purpose, for instance bone meal which supplies phosphorous at planting time, it is generally better to apply a combination of all three in a ready-mixed, compound fertilizer. The proportions of N, P and K vary from product to product, but should be indicated on the packaging. On the whole all-purpose formulas are inorganic, which means that they are manufactured products not of plant or animal ori-

gin. The nearest organic equivalent is fish, blood and bone. Generally speaking, organic fertilizers are slower acting than inorganics, and provide a steady supply of food over a long period so one application a year is usually enough Another advantage with organic fertilizer is that, since they work in conjunction with beneficial soil bacteria, more of the nutrients are released as the soil warms and plants come into active growth.

**WEEDS** A weed can be defined as any plant that is out of place. They have to be controlled because the compete with your chosen plants for water, soil nutrients and light, and will spoil the look of your planned border. Like cultivated plants, weeds can be categorized as annuals and perennials. Examples of annuals weeds include shepherd's purse and chickweed. These flower then spread around your garden by self-sowing. Perennial weeds include such horrors as bindweed, ground elder and couch grass, which all have underground storage organs enabling them to survive from year to year. For weed control, there are two choices – cultural control or chemicals.

For annual weeds, cultural control consists of hand-pulling or hoeing the weeds before they flower and set seed. Using weed killers on annual weeds entails the risk of contact with other cultivated plants, but for large areas it may be the only practical choice. With all weed killers that are applied as a spray or with a watering can, it is essential to choose a dry, still day when the danger of spray drift is minimal.

Ideally, perennial weeds should be eradicated from a bed or border before you plant it up, but they have a habit of returning. Perennial weeds in cultivated areas are usually controlled by a combination of both methods – cultural and chemical. Carefully forking out the shoots and roots, attempting to remove all fragments from the soil, will limit their spread, but applying a systemic weed killer during the growing season is usually necessary, too. The same precautions apply as for the control of annual weeds, as these chemicals will affect any plant they touch. Some types are available in gel form which is painted onto the weed leaves, or as a solid stick which is smeared on. Whatever product you choose, follow the instructions carefully.

# PLANNING FOR AROMA

If you go to all the trouble of selecting plants for their aromatic qualities, you want to be sure that you'll be able to appreciate their scent fully in your garden. If your garden is open and tends to be windswept, choose a sheltered area for your scented plants or introduce some form of screening as a wind break to prevent the perfume of your plants being blown away on the breeze.

A windbreak can take the form of a wall, fence, trellis, hedge or a group of trees. Walls, fences and trellis have the advantage of providing almost instant shelter, and will not take moisture and nutrients out of the ground nearby. Hedges and trees take time to grow, require maintenance and make demands on the soil, providing competition for the more choice plants that grow near them, but they are decorative. You could plant a windbreak of aromatic shrubs, so that the wind is scented before it filters into your perfumed garden.

Once you have created or chosen an area where the scents of your herbs and aromatics will be confined for your pleasure, you will need to get close to the plants to enjoy their perfume to the full. Paths running alongside your beds and borders will lead you right into the scented environment, allowing you to brush past aromatic foliage, to crush a scented leaf between your fingers or underfoot, or to lean into a border to enjoy the perfume of a taller plant.

A paved area in the scented garden can be enhanced by the addition of plants in containers that are swapped around in season to bring the most fragrant

*Such a lovely combination of colour, fragrance and shape is ideal for any garden except perhaps the smallest. However, if you have a small garden, try growing the variety* L. 'Pendulum', *which is ideal.*

*The beauty of so many bulbs is that they can be grown in any number of places to add colour and fragrance at any time of year, but perhaps particularly in the spring. Here is a glorious display of blue and white hyacinths, violas, yellow narcissi and polyanthus.*

specimens to the fore. In summer, the heat that reflects off hard paving can bring out the best in Mediterranean herbs, such as thyme, marjoram and rosemary, drawing the scented essences from their leaves to create a cloud of tangy scent. Add seating and a table if you have room, and you can grab a handful of herbs to add to your salad or toss onto the barbecue. If you eat dinner outside on your terrace, plant night-scented flowers nearby. Nicotianas, night-scented stocks, lilies and daturas will seem to glow in the dark and fill the air with a heady scent.

Containers are invaluable for growing less-hardy plants. They can be put under cover if there is danger of a frost and brought out into the open to be enjoyed when conditions are safe. Putting a plant in a container is equivalent to underlining it. It calls out for attention, and is the ideal position for a small, choice plant that might get lost in a border or one with a slight fragrance that deserves close attention, making it accessible to passers by.

As well as making sure you can get close to the plants, make sure they can get close to you, and to the bit of you that counts – your nose. Raised beds, as well as bringing the scent higher up, offer an opportunity to introduce plants that you would otherwise not be able to grow, since you can fill them with a different type of soil than that which you have in the rest of your garden. If your soil is alkaline, for instance, you could construct a raised peat bed and grow some of the beautifully scented azaleas that would otherwise die of lime-induced chlorosis in your garden, but don't forget to collect rain-water for irrigation. Many peat-loving plants have a high water requirement, and hard, limy water from the tap will turn acid-lovers yellow in no time.

Hanging baskets can be filled with scented plants and make a pleasing feature by a door or on a patio. At head level, they will allow you to enjoy a rich variety of aromatic plants that might pass unnoticed lower down. Remember to water at least once a day in summer, and never to let a hanging basket dry out completely. Once it does you will have to take it down and let it sit in a bowl of water for at least a few hours. Incorporating moisture-retaining gel granules in the planting mix is a good idea and will help to ensure that this never happens.

Make full use of scented climbers and you could create a spectacular vertical feature which will surround you with both scent and flower. An archway, pergola, bower or screen can be bought from a garden centre, ordered from specialised suppliers or even home made and smothered with climbers. Even in a small garden, the use of climbers can greatly increase the capacity for flowering and perfume, but don't neglect feeding and watering, particularly if the climber is planted at the foot of a wall.

Two excellent roses to include for a bower or near a path are the thornless Bourbon climbers, 'Zepherine Drouhin' and the paler pink, slightly less-vigorous sort, 'Kathleen Harrop'. Both are free flowering and

have a delicious raspberry scent. Otherwise, roses should be used with caution as the twining, thorny stems can present a hazard at face level. But there are plenty of other climbers to choose from. In the evening, the white or pink-tinged flowers of jasmine will add their rich scent from summer to early autumn, and honeysuckles can be planted in variety to provide an unforgettable perfume starting late spring and continuing into mid-autumn. With a seating area incorporated, you can enjoy a romantic treat for the senses that will be the envy of everyone who visits your delightful aromatic garden.

*A traditionally designed herb garden in the world-famous Kew gardens presents a picture of perfection. Neatly laid out beds incorporate many different herbs using the low growing types to box in the taller varieties in the middle.*

# PROPAGATION

**SEEDS** Raising plants from seed is the economic way to stock your garden. Hardy annuals can be sown outside in late autumn or spring. The ground should be clear of weeds, raked to a fine tilth and watered, if dry. Sow in drifts marked out with silver sand for a natural look, in shallow drills to make weeding easier once seedlings emerge. Rake soil over the seeds and cover with brushwood to protect seedlings from birds.

Half-hardy annuals should be raised indoors in seed trays or pots, in a special seed or all-purpose compost. Firm compost down, making sure it is level and water well. Sow the seeds and cover with a little compost. Cover with polythene or a sheet of glass until the seedlings emerge. Prick the seedlings out once the first set of true leaves appear, and they are large enough to handle, but hold them by the seed leaves. Grow them on, gradually hardening off and transfer to their flowering position once the danger of frost is past. Hardy perennials can also be raised from seed, following the half-hardy method, and may flower in the first year.

## BULB OFFSETS AND SCALES

Bulbs and corms propagate themselves without any assistance if they are happy in their position, by producing smaller versions which will grow to flowering size in anything up to three years. You can improve the quality of these offsets and cormlets by removing them from the parent and planting them separately where they have more space and food. Some lilies can be propagated by lifting the bulbs, removing some of the outer fleshy scales and planting them at half their depth in warmth. Roots will form and a tiny bulb develops at the base of the scale. This is grown on and should flower in about three years.

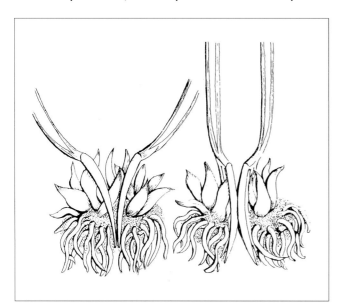

## ROOT DIVISION

This is a simple method for increasing your stock of fibrous-rooted perennials, including marjoram, fennel, chives, primulas and hostas. It can be carried out at any time during the dormant season, but best results are obtained by waiting until early spring, when the plant is just coming into growth. Dig up the plant and split the clump into two or possibly more sections using two garden forks back to back, or by hand if it yields easily. If the clump is old, the outer, younger parts will usually give better results. Replant the divided clumps immediately.

## CUTTINGS

The main types of stem cutting are basal, semi-ripe and hardwood. The first method is useful for increasing herbaceous plants. Basal cuttings are removed from the parent plant in spring. They should be at least 5cm/2in long and are cut or broken off as low down as possible to include part of the root clump of the plant. They are easily damaged and should be potted up quickly, and covered with polythene to prevent them drying out. They should root in a few weeks, and can then be hardened off.

Semi-ripe cuttings are green at the tip and starting to harden up at the base. They are usually taken from midsummer to autumn. This method is used for shrubs including lavender, daphne, rosemary and lilac. The cutting is usually 10-15cm/4-6in long, and either cut below a leaf joint, or taken as a heel cutting – a side shoot removed from the main stem with a sliver of bark attached. The soft tip can be pinched out, and greater success is achieved by dipping the cut end in hormone rooting powder before inserting to about a quarter of its length in a free-draining compost. It will have rooted by the following spring, but may not be ready for planting out until the autumn.

Hardwood cuttings are generally very successful, and are a useful way of propagating deciduous shrubs in the dormant season. They are taken after leaf fall and should be about pencil thickness, and 20-25cm/8-10in long. Make a slanting cut above a bud at the top, and a straight cut below a node at the bottom. Dip the bottom in hormone rooting powder and insert in well-drained soil to leave about a third of the cutting above ground. The cuttings should be ready for planting out in about a year. For all cuttings, it is vital to make sure that the stock from which you are propogating is disease free, and that your secateurs or knife, pots and trays are kept scrupulously clean.

# PRUNING

Although plants in the wild survive quite happily without being pruned, in the garden most shrubs and trees are regularly cut back for a number of reasons. Pruning improves flower display by encouraging the plant to produce more and better blooms; it limits the size of shrubs and maintains a tidy appearance; it improves the vigour and health of a plant through the removal of dead or diseased wood. The fact that different plants need to be pruned at different times of year seems confusing at first, but it is actually quite logical, and relates to the habit of the plant. There are two main groups.

The first consists of shrubs that flower on the current season's wood, usually rather late in the year, from late summer to autumn. These include Buddleia

# LAYERING

This technique can be used for border carnations, clematis, honeysuckle, rosemary and sage. The shoots of these plants will grow roots if buried in the ground while still attached to the parent plant. Layering should be carried out between spring and late summer when the plant is in active growth and the soil is warm. Young stems take best, and can be helped along by wounding, or cutting a slit about halfway through the stem at an angle. Bury the shoot with the cut portion at the bottom and peg it down in the soil with a piece of wire, making sure the end of the shoot is projecting from the soil. Water regularly and in about six months for carnations, or a year or two for shrubs the root system of your layer should be well developed. Once you have checked that this is the case, the shoot can be cut away and planted up on its own.

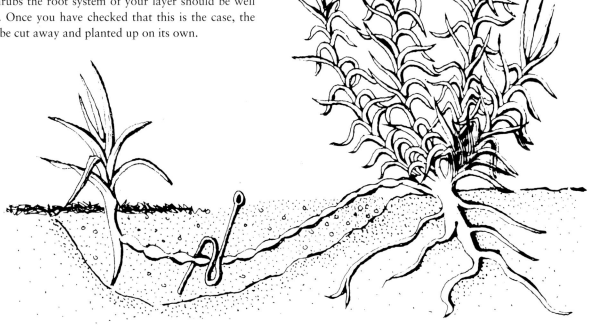

davidii, fuchsias, passiflora, santolina, lavender, bush roses and the large-flowered clematis, such as 'Jackmanii', that flower after mid-summer. These should be pruned in spring as growth is beginning, then fed with a general fertilizer and mulched.

The second is made up of shrubs that flower on wood formed the previous year. They include philadelphus, forsythia and weigelia. These should be cut back after flowering so that the new wood produced has time to ripen that same year for flowering the next.

Slow-growing deciduous shrubs, like daphnes, azaleas and lilacs need no regular pruning, apart from the removal of weak or diseased wood. Evergreens and conifers need no pruning, except an occasional trim to keep them neat. If grown for hedging, however, more regular attention is needed.

As a general rule, ensure secateurs are sharp and clean, and clear up all prunings straight away.

ON THE SCENT - PLANT NAMES THAT INDICATE FRAGRANCE  All the plants listed in this book have been selected for their fragrance, either of flower or leaf, but there are many more with wonderful aromas. The common name of a plant often tells you something about it's characteristics, but so may the Latin name, particularly the species name, usually the second word of the botanical title. For example, sweet sultan is a well-know scented annual, but it's Latin name, *Centaurea moschata*, tells you more – *moschata* means 'musk-scented'. As you look through catalogues or plant lists, look out for the species name. There are some that refer quite specifically to scent.

Acris - acrid, pungent

Aromatica, aromaticum - aromatic

Balsamea - fragrant

Carophyllus - clove-scented

Cinnamomea - cinnamon-scented

Citriodora, citriodorus - lemon-scented

Fragrans - sweetly-scented

Graveolens - strong-smelling

Moschata, moschatus - musk-scented

Odora, odorata - highly-scented

Odoratissimus - very highly-scented

Roseum - rose-scented

Suavis, suavolens - sweetly-scented.

16

# PLANT FINDER

## PLANTS FOR SHADE

**HERBS** *Bergamot, Parsley, Mint, Sweet Woodruff*
**ANNUALS AND BIENNIALS** *Asperula, Malcolmia, Nicotiana*
**BULBS, CORMS AND RHIZOMES** *Cardiocrinum, Convallaria, Cyclamen, Smilacena*
**PERENNIALS** *Hosta, Houttuynia, Phlox, Primula,*
**ROSES** *Rugosas, Albas, Damasks, Gallicas,* ·
**SHRUBS** *Deutzia, Gaultheria, Osmanthus, Rhododendron*
**TREES AND CLIMBERS** *Lonicera, Stuartia,*

## LIME-TOLERANT PLANTS

**HERBS** *Helichrysum, Lavender, Sage, Thyme*
**ANNUALS AND BIENNIALS** *Centaurea, Cheiranthus, Dianthus, Scabiosa*
**BULBS, CORMS AND RHIZOMES** *Crocus, Iris, Muscaris, Tulipa*
**PERENNIALS** *Achillea, Dianthus, Dictamnus, Perovskia*
**ROSES** *Albas, Ramblers, Rugosas, Sweetbriars*
**SHRUBS** *Buddleia, Myrtus, Philadelphus, Syringa*
**TREES AND CLIMBERS** *Clematis*

## PLANTS FOR CONTAINERS

**HERBS** *Basil, Bay, Nasturtium, Parsley*
**ANNUALS AND BIENNIALS** *Alyssum, Datura, Malcolmia, Reseda*
**BULBS, CORMS AND RHIZOMES** *Acidanthera, Hyacinthus, Lilium, Narcissus*
**PERENNIALS** *Hosta, Pelargonium, Verbena*
**ROSES** *Miniature, Patio and small-Cluster-flowered types*
**SHRUBS** *Daphne, Escallonia, Myrtus, Rhododendron*
**TREES AND CLIMBERS** *Clematis, Lonicera, Passiflora, Wisteria (Grown as a standard)*

KEY TO SYMBOLS

FLOWERING PERIOD — DEGREE OF HARDINESS — PREFERRED POSITION — EVERGREEN

MAXIMUM HEIGHT — MAXIMUM SPREAD — DISTANCE BETWEEN PLANTS — DISTANCE BETWEEN ROWS

CONTAINER — SMALL PLOT OR CONTAINER — SMALL PLOT — SOWING OR PLANTING DEPTH — HARVEST TIME

# PESTS AND DISEASES

## PESTS

| PROBLEM | DAMAGE CAUSED | REMEDY |
|---|---|---|
| Aphids (greenfly,blackfly) | Sap sucked; honeydew emitted, virus diseases spread | Spray with pirimicarb |
| Capsid bug | Leaves tattered or with tiny holes | Spray with systemic insecticide |
| Caterpillar | Leaves, stems, flowers eaten | Spray with permethrin |
| Earwig | Flowers, shoot-tips, young leaves eaten | Trap with straw-filled inverted flowerpots on canes among plants; kill with malathion or HCH |
| Eelworm | Plants weakened, leaves and stems distorted | Destroy infected plants, do not grow again on same site |
| Froghopper | Sap sucked under cuckoospit | Spray with fenitrothion |
| Leaf miner | Pales tunnels in leaves | Remove infested leaves; spray with pirimphos-methyl |
| Lily beetle | Leaves eaten | Spray with pirimphos-methyl |
| Mealy bug | Sap sucked, virus diseases spread by small insect enclosedin white 'wool' | Spray with Malathion |
| Narcissus fly | No flowers; weak, grassy leaves; maggots in bulbs | Destroy infested (soft) bulbs |
| Red-spider mite | Sap sucked; foliage desiccated; fine webs spun | Spray with fenitrothion or malathion |
| Rhododendron bug | Leaves mottled, yellow above and brown below | Spray leaf undersides with pirimphos-methyl |
| Sawfly | Leaves eaten or rolled under | Spray in late spring with pirimphos-methyl |
| Scale insects | Sap sucked, virus diseases spread by small, limpet-like insects | Spray with malathion |
| Slugs and snails | Young plant leaves eaten | Scatter methiocarb thinly among plants |
| Thrips | White speckles, then grey patches on leaves, flowers | Spray with fenitrothion |
| Vine weevil | Lower leaves holed and notched; grubs on roots, plants wilt | Dust lower leaves and soil with HCH |
| Whitefly | Sap sucked; virus diseases spread | Spray with permethrin |

## DISEASES

| | | |
|---|---|---|
| Azalea gall | Hard green reddish or whitish swellings on leaves and buds | Cut out and burn infected stems; spray with copper fungicide |
| Bacterial canker | Leaves full of holes; stem cankers with oozing gum; general weakening | Cut out infected wood; spray with benomyl |
| Blackspot | Rose leaves develop black spots, fall early | Rake up and burn all leaves at end of season; spray with bupirimate and triforine |
| Botrytis (Grey mould) | Parts of plants rot, become covered in grey fur | Remove and burn infected parts; spray with benomyl |
| Bud blast | Rhododendron buds turn brown, develop black pinhead spore capsules and fail to open | Cut off infected buds; spray with fenitrothion to control leafhoppers that spread the disease. |
| Canker | Rough brown sunken areas on stems | Cut out and burn; spray with thiophanate-methyl |
| Chlorosis | Leaves yellowed; growth stunted on alkaline soils | Grow plants on acid soils. Water with iron sequestrene; feed well |
| Clematis wilt | Collapse of mature shoots, usually on young plants | Cut back to ground level; water with benomyl |
| Coral spot | Raised orange pustules on woody stems | Cut out infected wood and burn; paint wounds with sealant |
| Die-back | Woody stems die at tip | Cut out infected wood back to healthy tissue |
| Fusarium wilt | Lower leaves and stem bases turn brown and rot | Destroy infected plants; do not grow species again on same ground |
| Honey fungus | Stems die back (or plants even die) for no visible reason. Fungal 'bootlaces' found in soil; honey-coloured toadstools on site | Dig up and burn infected plants; dig up all tree stumps Water with fungicide |
| Leaf spot | Dark blotches on leaves | Spray with copper fungicide in spring. Prevent by growing on good soil |
| Lilac blight | Black spots on leaves; shoots wither | Cut out infected wood; spray with bordeaux mixture |
| Petal blight | Petals covered by translucent spots, especiallly in wet weather | Remove and destroy infected blooms |
| Root rot | Roots turn brown and rot, killing plant | Destroy infected plants |
| Rust | Yellow spots on upper leaf surfaces, orange pustules below | Destroy infected plants; spray others with mancozeb. Prevent by growing resistant strains |
| Virus diseases | Leaves distorted, marbled, yellowed; plant often stunted | Dig up and burn; control insect disease carriers |

# HERBS

tainers, under conditions that few other plants would tolerate. Whatever their other characteristics, herbs are always interesting to grow, and all will enhance your food with a freshness of flavour that cannot be equalled. No garden, however small, should be without a few examples of these undemanding plants.

Growing herbs is a time-honoured tradition, with the earliest documented accounts of their use dating back to 2000BC in Babylon. There are plenty of historic physic gardens still in existence, often attached to monasteries and a visit to one of these can be quite an inspiration in establishing a garden or bed devoted solely to herbs. The earliest examples were strictly utilitarian, and used not only as a source of culinary interest but for cosmetics, medicaments and perfumes. The decorative aspect, therefore, was not of prime importance. In growing herbs today, a relaxed approach to choosing your plants will ensure that your herb garden is as attractive as the ornamental areas of your garden.

**A herb can be defined as any type of plant — annual, bulb, perennial or shrub — grown for its medicinal qualities or, more commonly nowadays, for its aroma and the subtle flavour it lends to food.**

Herbs, because of their diversity, range in size, shape habit and just about any other characteristic you can think of, with such extremes as the perennial angelica, a giant at 1.8m/6ft or more, and the lowly, but no less fragrant shrub Creeping Thyme, at 1cm/½in. Yet most herbs thrive in the same conditions, so they can be grouped together in a special herb garden that, with some planning, will be a delight at all times of year.

Some, although admittedly not all, are sufficiently ornamental to earn a place in ordinary garden borders, and many are hardy enough to survive in pots and con-

**CHOOSING AND PLANTING HERBS** For obvious reasons, culinary herbs should be grown within reach of the kitchen, but situation has to be considered. In general terms, herbs thrive in an open, sunny position, although parsley and mint are notable exceptions that will happily take some shade. Well- drained soil of reasonable quality gives good results with the richly aromatic Mediterranean genera, but some of these, such as the shrubs rosemary and bay, can be frost tender and prone to wind scorch, so a certain amount of shelter is desirable. In areas of very heavy soil, or where space is limited, growing herbs in tubs and containers is a viable alternative

Many herbs, and not just annuals, grow well from seed. This is a very economic way of stocking your herb garden but not suitable for some of the shrubs, such as rosemary, thyme and bay, which are far better bought as container-grown plants. A wide choice of

*An attractive collection of herbs including, chives, marjoram and rosemary are well established in this herb garden.*

herbs is available at specialist nurseries, garden centres and many other outlets, and most are easily propagated by cuttings or division once they are established, so enlarging your stock need not be expensive.

A further consideration in growing herbs for the kitchen is that of pest and disease control. Fortunately, herbs tend to be healthy plants, and all the more so if they are grown in optimal conditions, but even so aphids and various types of fungal disease may appear in your herb garden. Choose chemical-free control, or select garden chemicals intended for use on crops, and follow the instructions carefully.

**HERB GARDENS**   A herb garden need not be a purely utilitarian feature. On the contrary, it can be extremely decorative, especially with a little planning and a modicum of understanding about the habits of the plants you have selected. The basic principles are the same as for planning an ornamental mixed border, with shrubs providing permanent structure while perennials, annuals and bulbs are positioned to act as star performers at their individual seasons of interest.

The choice of plants may be more restricted, but this does not necessarily make the planning any easier. In fact, a whole new set of criteria, based on the use you want to make of the herbs, are added to the normal gardening ones. When it comes to designing your herb garden, you can learn a great deal by visiting historic herb gardens, which were often arranged in large formal patterns, and this idea can be successfully scaled-down for domestic gardens. An impressive formal feature can be produced with symmetrical beds of herbs, divided by paths, perhaps in gravel or brick, and edged with chives, box or lavender.

The maintenance involved in this kind of herb garden should not be underestimated. Some herbs are far more vigorous than others, and it can be a constant battle to prevent more choice plants being swamped. The seed heads of some herbs can be just as decorative as their flowers, but in a formal herb garden watch out for self-sown seedlings that can spoil your carefully drawn-up plan. The annual borage and various members of the family *Umbelliferae*, such as fennel, dill, chervil and angelica are notorious for this, so unless you are harvesting flowers and seed-heads for use in the kitchen, dead-heading is a must.

**HERBS IN THE BORDER**  Certain herbs are decorative enough for inclusion in an ornamental border, and the softness of colour, both of flower and foliage, that is characteristic of many herbs means that they are a useful foil for more showy plants, as well as blending perfectly with, for example, old-fashioned roses and other more restrained plants. The position of herbs in the border is important. Unless including them solely for their decorative effect, it makes sense to plant them near the front of the border where the leaves can be brushed by passers-by, so that the aroma can be appreciated as an integral part of the plant's charm.

**HERBS IN CONTAINERS**   Some herbs can be grown in containers very successfully. Half barrels, old sinks and troughs, strawberry pots, window boxes and even hanging baskets can be pressed into service to provide you with a supply of fresh herbs. The maintenance involved can be considerable, because of the frequency of watering and feeding that will be necessary and some herbs can become pot-bound so need to be transferred to a larger container. Changing the soil, as the nutrients get depleted, is a major task. However, the larger the container, the easier the cultivation.

In a limited space, the choice of plant is even more crucial, but there are plenty of compact, decorative and useful herbs that are perfect for growing in containers. In a cold climate, slightly tender herbs grown in pots can be moved under cover in the winter.

# ANTHEMIS

| small plot | summer | full sun | 23cm/9in | 37cm/15in |

*Anthemis nobilis* is the name for the perennial plant more commonly known as chamomile. A member of the daisy family – *Compositae* – all species bear small daisy-like flowers of white, cream, yellow or orange. The exception is the flowerless variety 'Treneague', which is the one most suitable for an aromatic lawn or path. The apple-banana scent of the foliage drifts up when the plants are walked upon, and is most fragrant on summer evenings.

**PROPAGATION AND GROWING** For a lawn, set out young plants in any ordinary well-drained soil in spring 15cm/6in apart each way. A light mowing may be necessary once or twice during the summer. Flowering species for ground cover or window-boxes should be planted out from autumn to spring. Every autumn after flowering, cut down the old stems. To propagate, divide and replant the roots in the autumn or spring.

**VARIETIES** *A. cupaniana*: white flowers with bright yellow centres, grey-green fern-like foliage; *A. nobilis*: mat-forming, white flowers, mid-green foliage; *A. nobilis* 'Florae Plena' *(above)*, the double-flowered variety has the strongest scent. *A. n.* 'Treneague': flowerless variety.

**POSSIBLE PROBLEMS** Generally trouble-free.

# FEVERFEW

| summer | hardy | full sun | 45cm/18in | 45cm/18in |

Like chamomile, to which it is closely related, feverfew *Chrysanthemum parthenium (above)*, is a member of the daisy family. It is a short-lived perennial usually grown as an annual which bears white or yellow flowers. The light green, deeply cut leaves have a sharp aroma. As a wild flower, feverfew rejoices in the common name flirtwort. Disappointingly, however, old herbals recommend it not as a love potion, but as a mild laxative.

**PROPAGATION AND GROWING** Sow seed in spring in fertile, well-drained soil. A sunny site is best, but some shade will be tolerated. Seed germinates easily, so it is best to raise new plants each year.

**VARIETIES** 'Aureum': green-gold foliage, single white flowers; 'White Bonnet': double, white flowers. Dwarf varieties ideal for pots and window-boxes are sometimes listed under *Matricaria eximia*; they include 'Golden Star', 20cm/8in high, with clusters of round yellow flowers and 'Snowball', 30cm/12in, with neat round white flowers.

**POSSIBLE PROBLEMS** Earwigs; aphids, cutworms.

---

## ▦ PLANTING TIP

Anthemis cupaniana *is an excellent front-of-border plant, where it will form a neat mound of foliage and flowers, but it comes into its own if planted in a* container *or on a retaining wall, where its tumbling stems of daisy-like flowers are shown to full advantage.*

## ▦ PROPAGATION TIP

*Earlier flowering can be achieved by sowing the seeds in gentle heat in seed trays, about 3mm/⅛in deep. They will germinate in 10-14 days.*

# SWEET WOODRUFF

| early summer | hardy | semi-shade | 15-23cm/6-9in | 30-60cm/1-24in |

*Galium odoratum* syn. *Asperula odorata (above)*, was one of the herbs used in Tudor times for 'strewing'. When dried it smells of new-mown hay, and was mixed with dried mint, thyme, hyssop and chamomile and cast on the floor to release their fragrance when walked upon (and, more practically, to inhibit household vermin). Woodruff belongs to a huge and varied family of plants which includes two famous for their aroma – gardenias and coffee. This less exotic species has shiny green lanceolate leaves and bears clusters of small white flowers in early summer. Woodruff grows wild in British woodland; in the garden it is useful as ground cover.

**PROPAGATION AND GROWING** Set out plants in groups from autumn to spring, in moist soil. Woodruff will do well under trees. To propagate, simply divide and replant at any time from autumn to spring.

**VARIETIES** There are no named varieties.

**POSSIBLE PROBLEMS** Generally trouble-free.

# SWEET CICELY

| late spring | hardy | semi-shade | 60-90cm/2-3ft | 45cm/18in |

A herbaceous perennial, sweet cicely, *Myrrhis odorata (above)*, belongs to the family *Umbelliferae*, in company with parsley, coriander, dill and a long list of plants both decorative and edible. Since it may reach 1.5m/5ft in favourable conditions, sweet cicely is best situated at the back of the border or herb bed, carrying its white flowers aloft. A pleasant scent reminiscent of aniseed is emitted by the large, fern-like leaves which, like the hollow stems, are covered in soft hairs. As the plant ages, the stems redden and the flowers give way to long, black seeds. Use the leaves when stewing tart fruits as a sweetener, or add them to fresh fruit salads. Chew the seeds to relieve indigestion.

**PROPAGATION AND GROWING** Sow seed in early spring in any ordinary garden soil. Choose a sheltered spot in sun or semi-shade: sweet cicely is a good candidate for the wild garden as it self-seeds readily. Alternatively plants may be divided in the autumn. If you do not want the seeds and wish to contain the spread of the plant, remove the flowers as soon as they fade.

**VARIETIES** There are no named varieties.

**POSSIBLE PROBLEMS** Generally trouble-free.

## ORGANIC TIP

*Consider using ground-cover plants, such as woodruff, to smother weeds as an alternative to spraying with herbicide.*

## COOK'S TIP

*The sweet flavour of the green, unripe seeds of this plant enhances fruit salads and homemade ice cream. Use chopped or whole.*

# TANSY

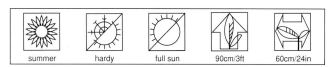

| summer | hardy | full sun | 90cm/3ft | 60cm/24in |

This old cottage garden favourite – *Tanacetum vulgare* (*above*), commonly known as buttons – is a member of the daisy family which bears flat clusters of small, yellow flowers at the top of long straight stems. A camphor-like fragrance resides in the large, deeply cut leaves, which have been used in many ways down the centuries, primarily as a tonic when infused in hot water. Tansy cakes used to be made at Easter, the slightly bitter leaves adding spice and bite to the mixture.

**PROPAGATION AND GROWING** A strong growing perennial, tansy can become a nuisance in the garden if left unchecked. Plant in any well-drained soil in spring or autumn. Remove flowerheads as they fade. Propagate by division in spring.

**VARIETIES** There are no named varieties, and alpine species of *Tanacetum* are not aromatic.

**POSSIBLE PROBLEMS** Generally trouble-free.

# HELICHRYSUM

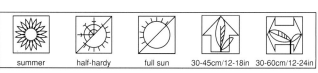

| summer | half-hardy | full sun | 30-45cm/12-18in | 30-60cm/12-24in |

Generally known as the everlasting flower, in fact only the annual helichrysum, *H. bracteatum*, merits the name. The aromatic member of the family is *H. angustifolium* (*above*), the curry plant, a bushy, slightly tender perennial with attractive silvery narrow leaves and clusters of small dull-yellow flowers. The whole plant smells of curry, which usually relegates it to the kitchen garden, although the foliage has a bitter taste and cannot be used in cooking. On a warm summer evening the aroma is intense and pervading.

**PROPAGATION AND GROWING** Plant in well-drained soil in full sun and sheltered from wind. The plant may be badly damaged by frost: better to cut it right back after flowering and protect with straw or leaf mould over winter. To propagate, take cuttings of side shoots in early summer.

**VARIETIES** There are no named varieties.

**POSSIBLE PROBLEMS** Generally trouble-free.

## ▨ ORGANIC TIP

*The bitter smell released when tansy leaves are crushed acts as a fly repellent. By tucking crushed leaves into their pockets, gardeners can keep flies at bay while they work outside, and a few fresh bunches laid in front of open windows will deter flies from coming in.*

## ▨ PLANTING TIP

*To get the best of the lovely curry scent, use as an edging plant near a path or seating area, where the plant can be brushed by people walking past.*

# MARIGOLD

| summer | hardy | full sun | 60cm/24in | 40cm/15in |

*Calendula officinalis (above)*, is the botanical name for pot marigold, a member of the daisy family with many traditional uses as a culinary and medicinal herb. It is a stalwart of the cottage garden – the roots are said to kill harmful soil bacteria and the smell of the leaves and flowers to discourage whitefly. The vivid orange-yellow petals add colour and pungency to salads; when dried, they can be used to colour savoury rice dishes.

**PROPAGATION AND GROWING** Marigolds are sturdy annuals that do well in cold climates and in towns. Sow seed in spring in well-drained, good soil, and thin the young plants to 45-60cm/18-24in apart. Remove flowerheads as they fade, leaving one or two on each plant if you want them to self-seed. The bushy habit of growth makes marigolds an ideal container plant.

**VARIETIES** 'Apricot Beauty'; 'Mandarin'; 'Orange King'.

**POSSIBLE PROBLEMS** Caterpillars; cucumber mosaic virus; powdery mildew; rust.

# LEMON BALM

| summer | hardy | semi-shade | 1.2m/4ft | 60cm/24in |

Lemon balm, *Melissa officinalis*, is a bushy herbaceous perennial suitable for mixed borders or to add height at the back of a bed devoted to herbs. It is also known as bee balm, *melissa* being derived from the Greek word for bee. Sprigs of balm are placed in the hive to contain bees when they are restless. The pale green, slightly hairy oval leaves can be used to decorate and add a hint of lemon to summer drinks; the dried leaves are sometimes used in pot pourri. The creamy-white blooms, like nettle flowers, are insignificant.

**PROPAGATION AND GROWING** Set out young plants in spring or autumn in any ordinary garden soil, in sun or partial shade. Cut stems right back in the autumn and protect the plant from frost in very cold districts. To propagate, divide established plants in the autumn.

**VARIETIES** 'Aurea' *(above)*, known as golden balm, with leaves splashed gold. When cutting back in autumn, leave the stems 15cm/6in long.

**POSSIBLE PROBLEMS** Generally trouble-free.

## PLANTING TIP

*Ideal for children to sow,* Calendula *can be in flower from mid-spring until the frosts, hence the Latin name, meaning 'throughout the months'.*

## SPECIAL CARE TIP

*Lemon balm is a vigorous perennial that may swamp weaker plants if unchecked. Keep a look out for unwanted self-sown seedlings.*

## SAGE

|  |  |  |  |  |
|---|---|---|---|---|
| small plot | full sun | 1cm/1.2in | 37cm/15in | 45cm/18in |

The green-leaved garden sage, *Salvia officinalis (above)*, primarily grown for its culinary uses, has a number of decorative forms, equally useful in the kitchen, which often feature in scented gardens. All are hardy, evergreen sub-shrubs of attractively bushy habit, reaching about 60cm/24in. The slightly bitter oval leaves can be used in any number of dishes, whether based on meat, fish, eggs or vegetables. They retain their flavour well when dried and in combination with onion are traditionally used as a stuffing for roast pork. In Tudor times, an infusion of sage leaves was prescribed for coughs and colds, for constipation, as a mouthwash and a hair conditioner – a versatile herb indeed. It is, after all, related to clary, the ancients' 'cure-all' and still used in perfumery.

**PROPAGATION AND GROWING** Sow seed in the open in late spring in a sunny position in well-drained soil. Remove flowers as they appear. Trim plants two or three times during the summer; they become leggy after a few years and should be replaced. Propagate from cuttings taken in early autumn.

**VARIETIES** Purple-leaved and variegated forms are recommended. *S. rutilans* or pineapple sage is a decorative plant bearing tubular scarlet flowers during the summer. The leaves smell of pineapple when crushed but have no culinary uses.

**POSSIBLE PROBLEMS** Generally trouble-free.

## JUNIPER

|  |  |  |  |  |
|---|---|---|---|---|
| evergreen | hardy | partial shade | variable | variable |

Numerous species of juniper, all evergreen, are cultivated as garden plants. *J. communis* is the one which bears edible berries; 3m/10ft high when mature, its needle-like leaves are grey-green with a white stripe. All parts of the plant are refreshingly aromatic. The berries are picked in their second year, when blue-black and ripe. They are used commercially in the making of gin. For cooking, the berries are first dried. A few crushed berries add distinction to pâtés, stuffings and marinades for game.

**PROPAGATION AND GROWING** Juniper does well on shallow, chalky soils and in seaside gardens. Set out young plants in late spring, in sun or partial shade. The species may be raised from seed sown in the autumn. Propagate named varieties by cuttings from side shoots taken in autumn.

**VARIETIES** *J. c.* 'Compressa': one of the smallest at only 45cm/18in after 10 years. Cone-shaped, with silvery leaves, it is ideal for inclusion in a trough of alpines. *J.c.* 'Depressa' *(above)*: low-growing, spreads up to 4m/14ft. *J. c.* 'Depressa Aurea' is a golden-leaved form. Both make excellent ground cover.

**POSSIBLE PROBLEMS** Scale insects; rust.

### ▨ SPECIAL CARE TIP

The forms with coloured foliage, like purple-leaved 'Purpurea', 'Icterina' with its yellow-edged leaves and 'Tricolor' with grey leaves marked with purple, white and pink, are not as hardy as the common form. They soon become scraggy and must be replaced regularly.

### ▨ PLANTING TIP

Because junipers vary so much in size, check carefully that the species and variety you buy is suitable for your planting position and garden.

# CHERVIL

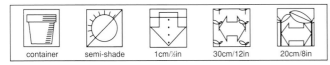

| container | semi-shade | 1cm/½in | 30cm/12in | 20cm/8in |

Chervil is related to parsley and is not dissimilar in flavour, though more delicate in appearance. Its botanical name is *Anthriscus cerefolium (above)*. Generous quantities are needed for cooking, particularly for delicious chervil soup. Like parsley, chervil is best used fresh, not dried, and makes a good accompaniment to vegetables and dishes based on eggs or cheese.

**PROPAGATION AND GROWING** A hardy annual, chervil is quick to germinate, and with successive sowing you can be sure of supplies all year. From early spring to late summer sow seed in any type of well-drained soil. Leaves can be picked once the plants have reached 10cm/4in. The mature height is about 45cm/18in. Protect the plants with cloches during the winter, or grow in pots and bring indoors.

**VARIETIES** There are no varieties of the species.

**POSSIBLE PROBLEMS** Generally trouble-free.

# RUE

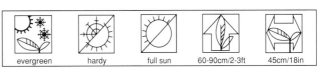

| evergreen | hardy | full sun | 60-90cm/2-3ft | 45cm/18in |

Because of its pungency, rue (*Ruta graveolens*) was included among the strewing herbs used to freshen fifteenth-century households, and in those days was much used in cooking. The flavour is too bitter for modern tastes, however, and it is now grown chiefly for its decorative value. Its blue-green leaves are deeply divided, the whole plant forming a neat rounded shrub. Acid yellow flowers appear in summer. Rue can be planted to form a low hedge, but if the old wives' tale is to be believed, it should not be sited around or near culinary herbs, to which it is supposed to be harmful. Rue looks wonderful in a sunny, mixed border, however, with no ill consequences.

**PROPAGATION AND GROWING** Plant from autumn to spring in well-drained soil in full sun. Trim back to old wood each spring to prevent the plants becoming leggy. Set plants for hedging 30cm/12in apart and pinch out the growing tips. Propagate by cuttings from side shoots taken in late summer.

**VARIETIES** 'Jackman's Blue' *(above)*: 45-60cm/18-24in high, suitable for containers, foliage brighter than the species, making a pleasing combination with silver-leaved shrubs.

**POSSIBLE PROBLEMS** Generally trouble-free.

## ▮ PLANTING TIP

*Chervil can be grown in a variety of containers, and is suitable for window boxes if kept well cut back, so that the plant remains bushy.*

## ▮ SPECIAL CARE TIP

*The sap of rue can cause skin irritation in some people, especially if the affected part is exposed to the sun. For this reason always wear gloves when trimming or propagating, and make sure that the plants are not directly next to a path where passers by may brush against them.*

## CARAWAY

| small plot | full sun | 2cm/¾in | 30cm/12in | 25cm/10in |
|---|---|---|---|---|

The graceful flowerheads of caraway, borne on top of 60cm/24in stems, identify it as a member of the parsley family, *Umbelliferae*. It is grown chiefly for its 'seeds' (actually fruits), which when ripe are added to cakes and bread or cream cheese. The leaves have something of their spicy aroma and are good freshly chopped and scattered over vegetable soups. The essential oil contained in the seeds is good for the digestion, and is released simply by chewing them. It is used in the liqueur Kummel. Caraway has been cultivated in Europe for centuries for medicinal purposes.

**PROPAGATION AND GROWING** Sow seed in early summer in light well-drained soil in a sunny position. Germination is swift. As biennials the plants reach maturity in the second year; in severe winters protect the seedlings with a mulch. Remove the seedheads before they burst open and dry them indoors. Dig up the plants at the end of the second year (sow every year for a continuous supply). The roots are edible – treat as carrots.

**VARIETIES** There are no varieties of the species, *Carum carvi (above)*.

**POSSIBLE PROBLEMS** Generally trouble-free.

## ANGELICA

| small plot | summer | semi-shade | 90cm/3ft | 90cm/3ft |
|---|---|---|---|---|

The edible parts of angelica are the hollow stem, which is candied for use in cakes and puddings, and the roots and leaves, which may be cooked with acidic fruits like rhubarb for a milder flavour. As a medicinal herb, it was used to make a soothing tea. Its decorative qualities are many, and at up to 2.4m/8ft high it easily merits a place at the back of a border where it will act as a windbreak for less sturdy plants. The mop-head white flowers which appear in early summer are coveted by flower arrangers – like all hollow-stemmed plants they will last a long time if the plants are up-ended and filled with water (hold your thumb over the stem end until you have placed them in the vase). All parts of the plant are pleasantly aromatic.

**PROPAGATION AND GROWING** Sow seed in late summer in the open ground and thin the seedlings to 15cm/6in in the first instance, thinning again if necessary. Alternatively start with a young plant and set out in spring. Although it is a biennial, angelica will keep going for several seasons if flowerheads are not allowed to form. The plants will take three or four years to reach maturity; if they flower the plants will self-seed very freely.

**VARIETIES** There are no varieties of the species, *Angelica archangelica (above)*.

**POSSIBLE PROBLEMS** Generally trouble-free.

### ▨ SPECIAL CARE TIP

*To make sure that no seeds are wasted, the seedheads should be hung upside down over a cloth in a dry room or shed until they drop out. Collect and store in an airtight container and they will keep for up to 6 months.*

### ▨ GARDENER'S TIP

*Angelica seeds have a short life, and will probably not germinate if you store them over winter for sowing in spring. Sow seed in autumn as soon as it is ripe; the seedlings are hardy enough to survive the winter. Unlike many herbs, Angelica thrives in a heavy soil.*

# MARJORAM

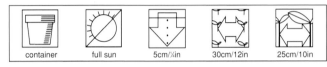

| container | full sun | 5cm/¼in | 30cm/12in | 25cm/10in |

Native to Europe, including Great Britain, marjoram was known to fourteenth-century herbalists, who recommended it in infusions for colds and sore throats. It belongs to the mint family, and the small rounded leaves have an aroma like thyme, but sweeter. Primarily a culinary herb, *Origanum majorana* – sweet marjoram, the best for flavour – is good with meat and stuffings for vegetables. It can also be used in pot-pourri.

**PROPAGATION AND GROWING** Treat sweet marjoram as a half-hardy annual. Sow seed under protection in early spring. Set out hardened-off plants in early summer in light but fertile soil in a sunny position. Sweet marjoram is useful for edging herb gardens or raised beds of aromatic plants. Perennial species can be increased by cuttings of basal shoots taken in spring.

**VARIETIES** *O. majorana*, sweet or knotted marjoram: a compact bushy plant 20cm/8in high; *O. onites* or pot marjoram: a hardy perennial with a strong aroma, at 60cm/24in it makes a small shrub for the herb bed; *O. vulgare*, common or wild marjoram, oregano: hardy perennial, up to 45cm/18in high; the decorative variety 'Aureum' *(above)*: has leaves splashed gold.

**POSSIBLE PROBLEMS** Generally trouble-free.

# BAY

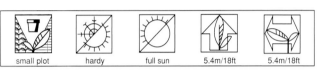

| small plot | hardy | full sun | 5.4m/18ft | 5.4m/18ft |

The leaves of the sweet bay, *Laurus nobilis (above)*, were used in ancient times to fashion a crowning wreath for heroes; in medieval times they were included among strewing herbs to sweeten and disinfect the house. In gardens of classical design immaculately clipped bay trees are an essential feature. As a culinary herb too, bay is indispensable, whether in a bouquet garni, added to the poaching liquid for fish, in stews and soups or even in rice pudding. An evergreen, its leaves have as much flavour in winter as in the height of summer, a rare quality among herbs.

**PROPAGATION AND GROWING** Set out young plants in spring on any type of soil. A sunny, sheltered spot is preferable – leaves are easily damaged by sharp winds. Most trees will reach about 3.6m/12ft in maturity if left alone. Specimens grown in tubs (of about 45cm/18in in diameter) should be pruned to shape during the summer. Propagate from cuttings taken in late summer, or by layering low-growing shoots.

**VARIETIES** There are no named varieties.

**POSSIBLE PROBLEMS** Scale insects.

## PLANTING TIP

*The basal leaves of pot marjoram form an evergreen mat during winter, making an attractive feature for the front of border.*

## SPECIAL CARE TIP

*Standard bay trees can be bought at great cost, but if you start early, perhaps with plants raised cheaply from cuttings, you can train them yourself, although it is a long-term project. Mature specimens in pots make an impressive, formal feature on a terrace.*

## COSTMARY

| autumn | hardy | full sun | 60-90cm/2-3ft | 45-60cm/18-24in |
|---|---|---|---|---|

Also known as alecost or herb st mary, costmary was one of the strewing herbs used to refresh Tudor households with its deeply penetrating scent of camphor. Correctly listed as *Chrysanthemum balsamita (above)*, it is a herbaceous perennial sometimes found as *Balsamita major* or *B. vulgaris*, and should not be confused with balsam (*Impatiens balsamina*, a half-hardy annual with large scarlet flowers). The daisy-like flowers of costmary are tiny, which may explain its rarity today. But the little blooms are numerous, the large elliptical leaves intensely aromatic, and at 90cm/3ft high costmary well deserves a place in a fragrant border.

**PROPAGATION AND GROWING** Plant from autumn to spring in fertile, well-drained soil. A sunny position is best, but some shade is tolerated. It is best to cut back after flowering. To propagate, divide established plants in autumn or spring.

**VARIETIES** There are no other varieties

**POSSIBLE PROBLEMS** Earwigs.

## BASIL

| container | full sun | 1cm/⅛in | 37cm/15in | 20cm/8in |
|---|---|---|---|---|

Basil is a half-hardy native of tropical zones which is best treated as an annual in cooler climates. It is a member of the mint family, highly esteemed by good cooks, and is best used fresh. Basil is an essential ingredient of the Genoese sauce *pesto* and the *soupe au pistou* of Provence. Tomato salad is not the same without it. The best culinary species is *Ocimum basilicum* or sweet basil *(above)* which reaches 60cm/24in or more with a spread of 30cm/12in.

**PROPAGATION AND GROWING** Sow seed indoors in spring. After a hardening-off period plant out in early summer in a warm, sheltered position in light, well-drained soil. Water when dry, but never saturate the soil. Remove the flowerheads as soon as they form.

**VARIETIES** *O. minimum* or bush basil: a dwarf form at 15-30cm/6-12in high, useful for container cultivation and with a good flavour.

**POSSIBLE PROBLEMS** Generally trouble-free in suitable conditions.

### SPECIAL CARE TIP

Although difficult to grow from seed in colder climates, costmary spreads rapidly once it is established. Older plants become straggly, so it is advisable, every 3 or 4 years, to discard them altogether and start again with new stock, which can be taken easily from basal cuttings.

### SPECIAL CARE TIP

Although perennial in warm climates, basil is frost tender. For a winter supply, lift from the garden in early autumn, disturbing the roots as little as possible. Pot them up using a well-drained compost, and grow on indoors on a sunny windowsill.

# MINT

| container | semi-shade | 5cm/2in | 30cm/12in | 15cm/6in |

The popularity of the mint family is undeniable; but all the mints are to varying degrees invasive, and will eventually take over the herb bed if left unchecked. Confine mint to tubs or boxes. If you want it in the garden, grow it in a submerged bucket with the bottom knocked out, or restrict the roots with slates buried vertically around them. In English kitchens, mint is traditionally used to make a sauce for roast lamb, or cooked with new potatoes. Mediterranean cooks, recognizing its beneficial effect on the digestion, are more adventurous – mint is used with many vegetables, in yoghurt as a dressing, with fish and salads and with fresh fruit.

**PROPAGATION AND GROWING** Set out rooted runners of this hardy perennial in spring in rich moist soil. Water well during the growing season and pinch out the tips to encourage a bushy shape. Plants are easy to raise by division in spring.

**VARIETIES** *Mentha spicata* or common mint, spearmint: 60cm/24in high, pointed leaves; *M. rotundifolia* or apple mint, Bowles' mint *(above)*: round-leaved variety, up to 90cm/3ft high, which is the the cook's favourite. Decorative mints include *M. citrata* or bergamot mint: 30cm/12in high, almost heart-shaped lemony leaves; *M. requienii*: prostrate, spreading, with tiny round peppermint-scented leaves.

**POSSIBLE PROBLEMS** Rust.

# LOVAGE

| semi-shade | 2cm/¾in | 60cm/24in | 60cm | 2-3 months |

Lovage deserves to be more widely grown by those who have the space. It is a handsome, bushy perennial plant with large but delicate light green leaves. At a possible height of 1.8m/6ft, it is best at the back of the border or providing shelter for smaller specimens. Yellow flowers appear in late summer. The leaves and stems have a celery-like flavour and can be used in any recipe calling for celery. Lovage soup is excellent, and the decorative leaves make a useful garnish. An infusion of the leaves is said to ease kidney ailments and reduce a fever.

**PROPAGATION AND GROWING** Sow seed in boxes of compost in autumn. Plant out seedlings in moisture-retentive soil the following spring. Leave one or two flowerheads on the plant and it will self seed readily. Alternatively collect seed as soon as it is ripe and treat as above.

**VARIETIES** There are no varieties of the species, *Levisticum officinale (above)*.

**POSSIBLE PROBLEMS** Generally trouble-free.

---

■ SPECIAL CARE TIP

*Mint takes a lot of goodness from the soil, so make sure you add plenty of compost at planting time, keep well watered for the best taste, and ensure that the soil is kept weed free. The plant should be moved to another site after 3 or 4 years, as this helps to avoid soil exhaustion.*

---

■ SPECIAL CARE TIP

*The young stalks of lovage are tender and can be eaten like celery. By covering the early shoots as they emerge in spring, using an inverted bucket or a large plant pot, they can be forced rather like rhubarb, and make an excellent addition to salads and crudités.*

HERBS

## Hyssop

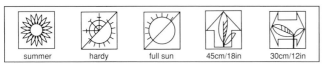

| | | | | |
|---|---|---|---|---|
| summer | hardy | full sun | 45cm/18in | 30cm/12in |

*Hyssopus officinalis (above)* has been prized as a useful herb for centuries – in the kitchen to preserve meat, as a remedy for coughs and colds and as a strewing herb. It is one of the herbal ingredients of the brandy-based liqueur, Chartreuse, and is also often included in pot-pourris. The small pointed leaves are pleasantly pungent, and the small flowers, which may be blue, pink or white, are sweetly fragrant.

**PROPAGATION AND GROWING** Hyssop is a decorative plant for the border, for pots, or as a low hedge. Though well-drained soil is preferred, it copes well with moist conditions. Plant from autumn to spring in a sunny position. Dead-head regularly, and cut the whole plant right back in spring. For hedges, set plants 23cm/9in apart and pinch out the growing tips to maintain a bushy shape. Trim lightly in spring. To propagate, raise plants from seed sown in spring, or take basal cuttings, also in spring, to ensure that the coloured varieties do not revert to blue.

**VARIETIES** As well as the pretty pink and white varieties, *H. o. rosea* and *H. o. alba*, there is a dwarf blue type, ideal for rock gardens, *H. aristatus*.

**POSSIBLE PROBLEMS** Generally trouble-free.

## Artemisia

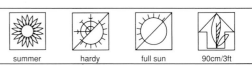

| | | | | |
|---|---|---|---|---|
| summer | hardy | full sun | 90cm/3ft | 90cm/3ft |

*Artemisia abrotanum (above)*, is a favourite of old cottage gardens, where it acquired its endearing common names of lad's love or old man. Also known as southernwood, this shrubby plant bears spherical, parchment yellow flowers in panicles over the summer; but it is grown for its silky, grey-green fine foliage, with an aroma both sweet and refreshing.

**PROPAGATION AND GROWING** Plant in spring on any ordinary garden soil with an open texture. Remove the flower stems when they fade. The plant dies down in winter. Pruning should not be necessary, unless to remove straggly growth in spring. Propagate from semi-hardwood cuttings taken in late summer.

**VARIETIES** *A. arborescens* or common wormwood is a slightly less hardy species which will, nevertheless, reach 1.8m/6ft against a sunny wall. The silvery foliage releases its fragrance when bruised.

**POSSIBLE PROBLEMS** Aphids; rust.

### ▌PLANTING TIP

*Hyssop is at its most fragrant in midsummer. If you grow it in a container, bring it near the house so you can enjoy the spicy scent.*

### ▌ORGANIC TIP

*Branches cut from the* artemisia *and laid between rows of vegetable crops are said to repel carrot and onion fly.*

# ROSEMARY

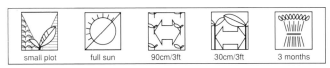

| | | | | |
|---|---|---|---|---|
| small plot | full sun | 90cm/3ft | 30cm/3ft | 3 months |

There is an old saying that rosemary will only grow in gardens 'where the mistress is master'. It is to be hoped that in these liberated times gardeners of all persuasions can find a place for it. Hardy almost everywhere, *Rosmarinus officinalis* or common rosemary *(above)*, reaches between 1-2m/3-6ft or more in height, making a dense, semi-erect bush of small, narrow dark green leaves which are intensely aromatic. Pretty pale blue flowers appear in early summer; if you are prepared to forgo them, rosemary can be clipped to make a hedge. The essential oil is an ingredient of eau de Cologne and many other perfumes; in aromatherapy it is used (with lavender) to relieve tension headaches. Because of its powerful aroma, rosemary should be used sparingly when cooking. Elizabeth David recommended basting charcoal-grilled fish with a rosemary branch dipped in olive oil (and finds no other use for it).

**PROPAGATION AND GROWING** Set young plants in a dry, sunny spot where they can be left to achieve full height. Cut back mature plants to half their height in the autumn to keep the shape neat. Increase by tip cuttings taken in summer.

**VARIETIES** 'Albiflorus': white flowers; 'Erectus' (syn. 'Fastigiatus'): upright form; 'Humilis': prostrate form spreading to 1.2m/4ft, syn. as *R. lavandulaceus*, not fully hardy.

**POSSIBLE PROBLEMS** Generally trouble-free.

# TARRAGON

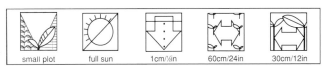

| | | | | |
|---|---|---|---|---|
| small plot | full sun | 1cm/½in | 60cm/24in | 30cm/12in |

Tarragon is a culinary herb of the genus *Artemisia*. There are two species for the kitchen garden: *A. dranunculus (above)* or French tarragon is far superior to Russian tarragon, *A. dranunculoides*, which is somewhat lacking in aroma; 'dranunculus', on the other hand, means 'dragon-like', which might as well refer to the sharp pointed leaves as to their incomparable flavour.

**PROPAGATION AND GROWING** Set out groups of young plants in good, well-drained soil in spring or autumn. Full sun is essential, and it is advisable to feed the plants during the growing season to achieve a good flavour. Pinch out the growing tips to encourage leaf development. As tarragon is a perennial: cut down the plants in late autumn and cover with straw to protect from frost. Divide and replant every 3 years in fresh soil, or treat as annuals.

**VARIETIES** *A. dranunculoides* lacks the sharp aniseed flavour of *A. dranunculus*.

**POSSIBLE PROBLEMS** Generally trouble-free.

---

## ▨ SPECIAL CARE TIP

*Although very hardy, in that it will thrive in hot, dry conditions, rosemary suffers in badly-drained soil and is damaged by cold winds and frost. In conditions less than ideal, it can be grown in a pot with gritty compost and moved to a sheltered position in cold weather.*

## ▨ SPECIAL CARE TIP

*Tarragon will suffer if planted on soil that has a tendancy to become waterlogged, and prefers an open, uncrowded situation. If your soil is heavy, plant it on a ridge or mound so that excess water can drain from around its roots, or try digging in some sand before planting.*

## FENNEL

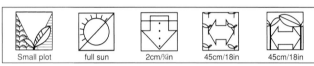

| | | | | |
|---|---|---|---|---|
| Small plot | full sun | 2cm/¾in | 45cm/18in | 45cm/18in |

Another member of the *Umbelliferae* family, fennel – *Foeniculum vulgare (above)* – is both highly decorative, with feathery bluish-green leaves, and very useful in the kitchen. The anise-like flavour is even stronger in the dried seeds than in the leaves. Like its close relative, dill, fennel is an aid to digestion. The leaves are best used to accompany fish vegetables and salads, the seeds in bread or soups. At 2.1m/7ft high this herbaceous perennial makes a stately addition to the border; it has been said that after a shower of rain a big bush of fennel looks like blue smoke.

**PROPAGATION AND GROWING** Sow seed in late spring, in well-drained, rich soil. If seed is not required, remove the flower-stems as they appear. Self-sown seedlings will appear freely if plants are allowed to flower; if not, propagate by dividing the parent plants every three years or so. The seeds are ready to harvest when they are grey-green and have hardened. Cut off the whole flowerhead and dry slowly indoors.

**VARIETIES** True green and bronze forms are available, much sought-after by flower arrangers. *F.v. dulce* is the vegetable Florence fennel, with similar foliage but grown for its swollen bulb-like stems.

**POSSIBLE PROBLEMS** Generally trouble-free.

## PARSLEY

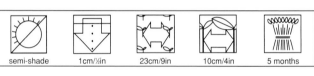

| | | | | |
|---|---|---|---|---|
| semi-shade | 1cm/½in | 23cm/9in | 10cm/4in | 5 months |

Parsley, *Petroselinum crispum (above)*, belongs to the *Umbelliferae* family, named from the umbel shape of the flower. It is one of the half-dozen most popular herbs and one of the few which good cooks insist on using fresh. It is an essential component of a bouquet garni, and in traditional cottage gardens was often used with alyssum as an edging plant. It attracts bees and is thought to repel greenfly.

**PROPAGATION AND GROWING** Sow seed outdoors in early spring in moist, rich soil. Parsley is notoriously slow to germinate; delay sowing for a few weeks and the warmer temperature will speed things along. Thin the seedlings to 20cm/8in. Water well in dry weather and cover with cloches if frost threatens. Later sowings, especially in pots that can be brought indoors, will provide leaves well into the winter. Although biennial, parsley is best grown as an annual and raised from fresh seed each year.

**VARIETIES** Curly-leaved parsley is the variety most often used for garnish, while the French or flat-leaved kind is said to have the better flavour. Plants may be low-growing or reach 60cm/2ft high. Turnip-rooted or Hamburg parsley, *P. c. fusiformis*, is grown for its celery-flavoured roots.

**POSSIBLE PROBLEMS** Leaf spot; discoloration caused by virus disease.

### ▦ ORGANIC TIP

*Fennel flowers attract beneficial insects to your garden. If allowed to prey on insect pests, they can help you avoid using garden pesticides.*

### ▦ PROPAGATION TIP

*You can help speed up germination by soaking the seeds overnight, or by watering in the newly sown seeds with hot water. Covering the seed bed with black plastic for 8 days after sowing will help maintain the warm, moist conditions that parsley needs to germinate successfully.*

# SALAD BURNET

|  |  |  |  |  |
|---|---|---|---|---|
| container | full sun | 45mm/1.4in | 30cm/12in | 30cm/12in |

Salad burnet, *Sanguisorba minor (above)*, can be found growing wild on grassland in Great Britain, particularly where the soil is chalky. It is a hardy perennial of the rose family forming a neat clump of foliage with many pairs of deeply toothed leaflets rather like those of a wild rose. The leaves have a pleasant cucumber-like fragrance, making them suitable for salads, as a garnish, or to float in cold drinks. They must be used fresh. Attractive rosy-lilac flowers appear on top of erect stems throughout the summer. Plants are variable in height, from 15-60cm/6-24in.

**PROPAGATION AND GROWING** Sow seed in late spring on light soil in sun or partial shade. When the flowers appear, pluck them off to encourage leafy growth. Burnet is wind-pollinated and self-seeds easily. It can be propagated by division but the flavour is better in plants raised from seed.

**VARIETIES** There are no named varieties.

**POSSIBLE PROBLEMS** Generally trouble-free.

# THYME

|  |  |  |  |  |
|---|---|---|---|---|
| container | full sun | 1cm/⅓in | 30cm/12in | 30cm/12in |

In any argument about the queen of herbs, you can count on a majority in favour of thyme. Maybe this is because there are so many that everyone can find a species of this evergreen shrub exactly to their taste. Once used as a strewing herb, and with medicinal applications ranging from a poultice for boils to a tonic bath or an ointment for insect bites, today thyme predominates in the kitchen. It is included in bouquets garnis, in stuffings, with vegetables, in omelettes and on pizzas. Place a sprig underneath a roasting joint or fowl. Dried thyme keeps its flavour well.

**PROPAGATION AND GROWING** Plant in spring in a sunny position in well-drained soil. Thyme is excellent in troughs, as an edging plant and for ground cover. Replace the plants when they become leggy. Propagate by division in spring.

**VARIETIES** *Thymus vulgaris* or common thyme *(above)*: height up to 20cm/8in, dark green narrow leaves, good flavour. *T.v.* 'Aureus' is an ornamental golden-leaved form. *T. × citriodorus* or lemon-scented thyme: height up to 30cm/12in, broader leaves; silver and gold-leaved forms are available. *T. herba-barona* or caraway thyme: mat-forming species, not fully hardy, traditionally used to flavour roast beef.

**POSSIBLE PROBLEMS** Generally trouble-free.

## ▨ PLANTING TIP

*Salad burnet is a very hardy plant, and the basal leaves stay green most of the winter, making it useful for decorative purposes.*

## ▨ PLANTING TIP

*The three species above are most commonly used in the kitchen, but there are many others of decorative interest. The creeping thymes,* Thymus serpyllum spp, *can be grown between paving stones, where the leaves and colourful flowers will release their scent when lightly crushed.*

33

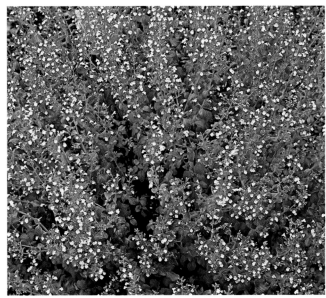

## SUMMER SAVORY

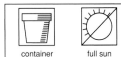   

| container | full sun | 1cm/1.2in | 23 cm9/9in | 15cm/6in |

The ancient Romans used the leaves of *Satureia hortensis* or summer savory *(above)*, to make a popular flavoured vinegar, and they believed the fragrance of the plant to be particularly attractive to bees. Since the leaves are soothing to insect bites, perhaps it is just as well the plants were often sited near the hives. The dark green leaves of this hardy annual are narrow and tapering, the plant bushy and upright to about 30cm/12in. Pale lilac flowers appear from the leaf axils throughout the summer. Savory is said to be a good growing partner for broad beans, acting as a repellent to blackfly. It is certainly a good companion to the beans once cooked, indeed with many bean dishes. The slightly spicy flavour gives it a place in bouquets garnis too, or boiled with new potatoes instead of mint.

**PROPAGATION AND GROWING** Sow seed in spring in fertile, well-drained soil in shallow drills, and thin to their final spacings when large enough to handle. For a winter supply, sow seeds in pots in late summer and keep at a minimum temperature of 7°C/45°F.

**VARIETIES** *S. montana* or winter savory; a perennial, almost evergreen sub-shrub, 30cm/12in high, grey-green foliage of inferior flavour.

**POSSIBLE PROBLEMS** Generally trouble-free.

## CALAMINTHA

| summer | hardy | semi-shade | 45cm/18in | 45cm/18in |

The minty aroma of *Calamintha grandiflora (above)*, is released by bruising the foliage. A cloud of tiny pink flowers covers the plant in summer, making it suitable for cottage gardens or for a 'wild' corner. According to some old herbals, a handful of crushed calamint leaves could be used to relieve cramp.

**PROPAGATION AND GROWING** This perennial is happiest in full sun on well-drained soil, but will do well in partial shade as long as the soil is not too moist. Plant in spring. The plant self-seeds, but can be divided in autumn if wished.

**VARIETIES** *C. alpina*: 10cm/4in high, light green leaves and mauve flowers on trailing stems, good for rock gardens.

**POSSIBLE PROBLEMS** Generally trouble-free.

## ▓ PROPAGATION TIP

*Summer savory produces self-sown seedlings which transplant well, while winter savory is best propagated from heel cuttings.*

## ▓ PLANTING TIP

*The species* Calamintha nepetoides *has a profusion of blue and white flowers, and is particularly suitable for a dry, chalky soil.*

# PENNYROYAL

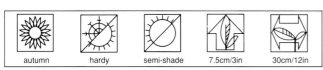

| | | | | |
|---|---|---|---|---|
| autumn | hardy | semi-shade | 7.5cm/3in | 30cm/12in |

Pennyroyal, *Mentha pulegium (above)*, is a mat-forming species of mint used in fragrant lawns, on paths or as carpet bedding. The aroma of its tiny rounded leaves is piercing rather than sweet and is released when they are crushed underfoot or brushed with the hand. Gardening lore has it that mints make a good growing companion for cabbages – perhaps the strong aroma with which the whole plant is imbued (roots included) keeps pests at bay. It is popularly supposed that the Latin name indicates its efficacy against fleas (for people, not cabbages, that is).

**PROPAGATION AND GROWING** Set out rooted runners in spring in rich moist soil, about 23cm/9in apart. Divide and replant in spring to propagate.

**VARIETIES** *M. p. gibraltarica* or Gibraltar mint; a compact variety with dark green, sometimes variegated leaves.

**POSSIBLE PROBLEMS** Generally trouble-free.

# LAVENDER

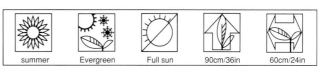

| | | | | |
|---|---|---|---|---|
| summer | Evergreen | Full sun | 90cm/36in | 60cm/24in |

Lavender is a shrubby plant which has been cultivated from ancient times for its refreshing perfume. It has medicinal as well as cosmetic uses. Smoothing lavender oil into the temples is wonderfully relaxing and a sure remedy for tension headaches; massaged into aching muscles (after gardening, perhaps), the oil eases stiffness. Lavender looks superb edging a rose bed or a pathway of brick or old flagstones. The flowers can be dried and used as a base in potpourri.

**PROPAGATION AND GROWING** Plant between autumn and spring on well-drained soil in full sun. Trim the plants back after flowering to prevent them becoming too leggy. For hedging or alongside a path, set plants 30cm/12in apart and trim in spring. To propagate, take cuttings of non-flowering shoots in late summer. Plants will sometimes self-seed.

**VARIETIES** *L. spica* or English lavender *(above)*: narrow, silvery leaves, spikes of purple-blue flowers. Recommended varieties include 'Hidcote', sweet scent, violet flowers; 'Folgate', late-flowering, leaves regularly spaced on the stems, blue-mauve flowers; 'Twickel Purple', finest fragrance. *L. stoechas* or French lavender: not fully hardy, overtones of mint to the perfume; large flower-spikes with lasting mauve bracts rise to 60cm/24in from a dense bush of leafy stems.

**POSSIBLE PROBLEMS** Frost damage; grey mould; honey fungus.

## ▪ PLANTING TIP

*Pennyroyal is an excellent choice for planting between stones by a pool or pond, where it benefits from the damp, cool conditions.*

## ▪ SPECIAL CARE TIP

*When cutting back lavender, be careful not to cut into the old wood, or new shoots will not appear. Yearly, light trimming, started when the plants are young, will ensure a compact, bushy shape. Old leggy specimens are best replaced as they cannot be cut back hard.*

# CHIVES

|  |  |  |  |  |
|---|---|---|---|---|
| container | full sun | 1cm/½in | 30cm/12in | 20cm/8in |

Chives are one of the most important culinary herbs, with a mild onion flavour. The chopped leaves can be used to garnish soups, salads and cooked vegetables, in omelettes or mixed with cream cheese. The narrow grass-like leaves grow in clumps up to 37cm/15in high. Pink pompon-shaped flowers appear in summer, pretty enough to qualify chives to be used as edging plants in a cottage garden (and, with luck, keep greenfly off the roses). For the best flavour, however, flower-heads should not be allowed to form. There is no reason why you should not grow some chives in the herb garden or in a tub for the kitchen and others for decorative purposes in the garden proper, allowing only the latter to come into flower.

**PROPAGATION AND GROWING** Chives may be raised from seed sown in shallow drills in spring and transplanted in early summer; or you can start with young plants and set them out in light, moisture-retentive soil. Water well in dry periods. Every few years, in the autumn, divide the clump into several sets and replant them in fresh soil. Chives do well in window-boxes or small pots, which can be kept indoors for a winter supply.

**VARIETIES** There are no varieties of the species, *Allium schoenoprasum (above)*.

**POSSIBLE PROBLEMS** Leaf-tips turn brown if the plant becomes dry.

---

### ▓ SPECIAL CARE TIP

*If you are intending to make extensive use of chives in the kitchen, make sure you have several clumps growing, and crop them in succession so that*  *you can take the tender, new growths every time.*

# NASTURTIUM

|  |  |  |  |  |
|---|---|---|---|---|
| summer | hardy | full sun | 24-38cm/10-15in | 10-20cm/5-10in |

This easily-grown annual herb, properly known as *Tropaeolum majus*, brings a splash of vivid colour to the herb border in summer, with its trumpet-shaped flowers in shades of cream, yellow, orange and scarlet. The flowers are only faintly scented, but the foliage and stalks are richly pungent when crushed. Both flowers and leaves can be eaten fresh in mixed salads and are a good source of vitamin C and iron. Their hot peppery flavour is a little like that of watercress. .

**PROPAGATION AND GROWING** Large, easily-handled seeds·make this an ideal plant for children to sow, and it is unlikely to disappoint. Sow seeds in pots or in the flowering site in mid-spring at a depth of 1cm/¾in. Grown in a sunny, open site in poorish soil, as a rich soil will lead to the production of leaves instead of flowers. Dead-head regularly to prolong flowering. Nasturtiums make excellent edging plants.

**VARIETIES** There are trailers, climbers and bush forms and a choice of single colours or mixed. 'Tom Thumb' is compact with single flowers in mixed colours; 'Alaska' has variegated leaves and flowers of mixed colours; and 'Whirlybird Scarlet' *(above)* are just a few of the many varieties.

**POSSIBLE PROBLEMS** Stems and leaves can be heavily infested by the black bean aphid.

---

### ▓ GARDENER'S TIP

*Try inter-planting nasturtiums with marigolds Tagetes tenuifolia (see page 42), which are very similar in colour and will make a most attractive display.*  *Also they are said to repel various insects, including aphids.*

# BERGAMOT

| Small plot | summer | semi-shade | 40cm/15in | 45cm/18in |
|---|---|---|---|---|

Bergamot, or *Monarda didyma (above)*, belongs to the *Labiatae* family, which also includes the mints, lavender, rosemary and thyme. It distinguishes itself in such famous company by its spectacularly colourful flowers of red, pink, white or purple. The dried leaves are used in pot-pourri, but the whole plant is impregnated with a delightful fragrance. Its attraction for bees gives it the popular name bee balm; in the USA it is called Oswego tea, after the American Indians who used it for a relaxing aromatic brew.

**PROPAGATION AND GROWING**  Because bergamot is shallow rooting it must be kept moist at all times. Start with young plants and set them out in clumps in spring or autumn – single specimens look lost in a border. Mulch with moisture-retaining material such as peat or leaf mould and provide short stakes. These hardy herbaceous perennials reach 60cm-1m/2-3ft but die down in winter. For a more colourful display, do not allow the plant to flower in the first season. To propagate, divide the clumps in spring.

**VARIETIES**  'Cambridge Scarlet'; 'Croftway Pink'; 'Snow Maiden'; 'Blue Stocking'.

**POSSIBLE PROBLEMS**  Generally trouble-free.

# BORAGE

| Small plot | Full sun | 2cm/¾in | 30cm/12in | 30cm/12in |
|---|---|---|---|---|

Like many plants with deep blue flowers, *Borago officinalis (above)* – a member of the forget-me-not family – is very attractive to bees. The flowers are seen to best advantage when grown in clumps,and as they may reach 90cm/3ft some form of support may be necessary for the stems. Borage earns a place in the herb garden because of its leaves, which have a refreshing cucumber-like taste. They can be used in salads, and are ideal to decorate a cool summer drink.

**PROPAGATION AND GROWING**  Sow seeds in spring where they are to flower in any ordinary well-drained, garden soil. Successive sowing will ensure a supply of leaves through the summer. The leaves should be ready for use within 6-8 weeks and should always be used perfectly fresh. Propagation of this hardy annual is easy – borage self-seeds very freely and may become a nuisance if not kept in check.

**VARIETIES**  There are no named varieties.

**POSSIBLE PROBLEMS**  Generally trouble-free.

## ▨ PLANTING TIP

*Bees are invaluable as pollinators in the garden, particularly if you have fruit trees. Encourage them by planting a bee garden, with plenty of bergamot, thyme, sage, rosemary, lavender, mint and catmint. They prefer single to double flowers.*

## ▨ COOK'S TIP

*The pretty blue flowers of borage make a very attractive decoration. Add to salads or fruit puddings. Alternatively, crystallize and use on top of cakes.*

# Annuals and Biennials

**Annuals and biennials, easily grown from seed, provide some of the most colourful displays in the garden, and many are remarkable for their scent.**

True annuals complete their life cycle within a year of being sown. Hardy annuals can be sown outside where they are to flower, half-hardy annuals are raised in heat, then transplanted to their flowering position when the danger of frost has past. Biennials take two years from sowing to complete their life cycle, and may be sown in the summer of one year to flower the next. To confuse the definition, however, some plants that are grown as annuals or biennials are actually short-lived perennials. This is the case with pansies, for example, or sweet williams which can be left in the ground to flower in subsequent years, but which will deteriorate in quality.

This group of plants is extremely useful in the garden. Annuals flower for a long period, given the right conditions, at minimal cost. Biennials are usually planted in their flowering positions in late autumn for the following year, and therefore provide some interest throughout winter. They tend to flower earlier than spring-sown annuals and fill in the gap between early spring bulbs and the summer show of perennials and annuals. Despite this, they are often under-valued by gardeners, perhaps because they seem so undemanding. Yet growing annuals and biennials really well takes quite a bit of time, thought and attention, and they will reward the right kind of care with a display of flower and scent that no other group of plants can match.

**BUYING AND SOWING** Choosing annuals and biennials is a perfect activity for the depths of winter, either browsing through a seed catalogue or leafing through the seed packets in a garden centre. Most annuals need a sunny, open position, although there are some notable exceptions. Biennials will thrive as long as they are in sun for part of the day. Apart from that, the main choice will probably hinge on size, and there are annuals and biennials to satisfy every need in that respect, from tiny edging plants suitable for the very smallest window box, through tall, stately specimens for the back of borders, to fast-growing climbers that will scramble up fences and trellising or into trees in a single season.

There is plenty of scope for choosing annuals and biennials for their scent, but the size and showiness of a flower is no guide to how fragrant it will be. Some of the most nondescript looking flowers yield a perfume that can be detected at a distance, particularly in the evening.

Hardy annuals are sown directly where they are to flower, usually in spring, although some of the hardier genera can be sown the previous autumn and will flower earlier the following year as a result. Extreme conditions are best avoided when sowing — neither wet, sticky soil nor bone dry is desirable. It should be possible to rake the soil to a fine crumb texture to make the seed bed. A neutral to slightly alkaline soil gives the best results, and lime can be added to an acid soil if necessary. A light top-dressing of fertilizer will help the seedlings establish, but heavy feeding should be avoided, as it may lead to excessive leafy growth and relatively little flower. For a whole bed of annuals, sowing in drifts gives the most natural result. Irregular shaped areas can be marked out with silver sand, then shallow drills formed for the seed to be sown in. The drills can then be covered, and the soil on top gently firmed. Sowing in drills, although it takes longer than sowing broadcast, makes weeding much easier once the seedlings begin to emerge.

As the annuals develop, it may be necessary to thin them out to prevent overcrowding. Taller annuals often need support which can be provided by pushing twigs into the ground between rows when the plants are still quite small.

Many of the same considerations apply to raising biennials and half-hardy annuals, *(see page 14)* although it is becoming increasingly easy to find a wide variety of good quality, well-grown bedding plants, as they are also known, in garden centres, ready to plant. No matter how you start your plants off, aftercare is all-important. Water well in periods of drought. Pinch out the growing tips of young plants to help to make them bushy as they mature, and dead-head to remove faded flowers before they produce seed, so as to prolong the flowering season. If the seed heads are decorative, of course, they will be left to develop, but flowering will cease early. Some annuals will self-seed, and in an informal garden this can give delightful results, but if you want to prevent it, dead-heading is vital.

**IN THE GARDEN** With new seed varieties being developed all the time, the choice of annuals, both hardy and half-hardy, and biennials is huge. In every colour, size and shade, the problem is knowing where

*A bed of half-hardy annuals making a stunning show in high summer. Including* Tagetes signata *(see page 42 left, front) and African and French marigolds in the background.*

to stop. Annuals and biennials play a unique role in the garden. No other type of plant gives such a display for so little cost, so for gardeners on a tight budget, they are indispensable. In a brand new garden, where decisions still have to be made about permanent features, they are the obvious stop-gap, and in newly planted borders they fill up space temporarily that shrubs and perennials will eventually grow to occupy. This is not to say that there is no place for annuals in an established garden, far from it.

The fragrant annuals and biennials listed in this chapter are so adaptable that space should always be reserved for them, either exclusively or in a mixed border, where they will survive quite happily as long as there is not too much competition for light and water. With their ability to scent the air, day and night, they earn a place near to paths, in raised beds and containers, under windows, on patios, on trellises and arbours, and around garden seating features. Anywhere that scent and flower are required from spring until the autumn frosts is the right place for these easy, appealing, undemanding and ultimately rewarding plants.

# DATURA

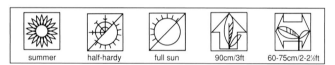

| | | | | |
|---|---|---|---|---|
| summer | half-hardy | full sun | 90cm/3ft | 60-75cm/2-2½ft |

*Datura ceratocaula* and *D. meteloides* are annuals that, in temperate climates, must be raised under glass for flowering in a cool greenhouse or as container-grown patio plants. Both have white, sometimes blueish-tinged, trumpet shaped flowers, about 15cm/6in long, and both are beautifully scented. *D. meteloides* is really a short-lived shrub, but is almost always treated as an annual. Both are wonderfully exotic looking, and are best grown as specimen plants – they would outshine most other plants.

**PROPAGATION** Seeds should be sown under glass in early spring, at 16°C/61°F. Prick out seedlings into individual pots, harden off if they are to be grown outside, otherwise pot on as needed. *D. meteloides* can be propagated by cuttings taken in late summer.

**GROWING** For growing outside, choose a sunny, sheltered spot in fertile, moisture-retaining soil. If grown in a greenhouse, provide shade and ventilation on hot days .

**VARIETIES** *D. inioxia (above)*; *D. meteloides* 'Evening Fragrance' has very large flowers with a lavender edge, and a bluish tinge to the foliage.

**POSSIBLE PROBLEMS** Red spider mite.

# HESPERIS

| | | | | |
|---|---|---|---|---|
| summer | hardy | full sun | 60-90cm/2-3ft | 45cm/18in |

Almost invariably described as a cottage garden plant, *H. matronalis* has a variety of common names all of which give a clue to its popularity for all types of garden. Sweet rocket, dame's violet or damask violet – take your pick. It is as fragrant whatever you call it, particularly in the evening. As a biennial, it flowers rather early in summer, even starting in spring, and the blend of colours, white purple and lilac, make a lovely soft effect in the herbaceous or mixed border.

**PROPAGATION** Sow seeds in mid-spring in a nursery bed, thin out and transfer to the flowering position in autumn.

**GROWING** A sunny position, with a fairly moist, alkaline soil is best. Dead-head to prolong flowering.

**VARIETIES** 'Alba' *(above)* is a white form.

**POSSIBLE PROBLEMS** Generally trouble-free.

## ▦ PLANTING TIP

*This is one of the plants that is even more perfumed at night. Try growing it in a conservatory or on a patio where you sit out in the evening.*

## ▦ SPECIAL CARE TIP

*Hesperis can be grown as a short-lived perennial and will give reasonable results in the second and third years, particularly if the site is suitable.*

## CENTAUREA

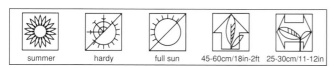

| | | | | |
|---|---|---|---|---|
| summer | hardy | full sun | 45-60cm/18in-2ft | 25-30cm/11-12in |

The best known annual centaurea is the cornflower, but *C. moschata*, or sweet sultan, is just as easy to grow from seed, has much larger flowers in a wider range of colours and has the added attraction of scent. Flowers are produced all through the summer and are excellent for cutting.

**PROPAGATION** Sow seeds in their flowering position in early autumn for larger plants and earlier flowering the following year, or in spring. Successive sowing will prolong the flowering season.

**GROWING** Choose a sunny site with well-drained, reasonably fertile soil. Thin seedlings in spring to give the correct spacing. Tall varieties may need staking, especially in an exposed site. Dead-head regularly to prolong flowering.

**VARIETIES** Mixed colours give pink, mauve, white, yellow, purple and dark red. For pure white flowers, sow 'The Bride' *(above)*.

**POSSIBLE PROBLEMS** Generally trouble-free.

## RESEDA

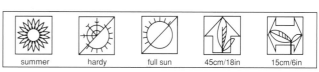

| | | | | |
|---|---|---|---|---|
| summer | hardy | full sun | 45cm/18in | 15cm/6in |

Do not be put off by the rather insignificant greeny-yellow spikes of tiny flowers – *R. odorata (above)* or mignonette is beautifully fragrant. The most usual way of including it in the garden is to interplant it with other, showier plants; indeed, its bright green leaves makes a good foil for some of the hot, bright colours of summer. It is equally suitable for sunny borders, containers and window boxes, but plant it near the house so that you, as well as the bees, can enjoy it.

**PROPAGATION** Sow in the flowering position in spring for summer flowering, or in autumn in mild areas for late spring flowers. Thin the seedlings carefully and do not allow the soil to dry out.

**GROWING** Plant in a sunny position, in an alkaline soil which should be reasonably well drained. If the soil is too rich, the plants will produce too much leaf and not enough flower.

**VARIETIES** 'Machet' and 'Crimson Fragrance' have been developed to give slightly showier flowers, but many gardeners feel that some of the fragrance has been lost.

**POSSIBLE PROBLEMS** Generally trouble-free.

## ▨ SPECIAL CARE TIP

*Thin seedlings before they become overcrowded. Do not neglect weeding and watering. Any check to the growth of young plants will delay flowering.*

## ▨ SPECIAL CARE TIP

*Sow mignonette in pots in early autumn to flower during the winter, when it can be brought inside the house and its fragrance enjoyed out of season.*

# ALYSSUM

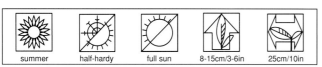

| summer | half-hardy | full sun | 8-15cm/3-6in | 25cm/10in |

Actually a dwarf perennial, *A. maritimum* is always grown as an annual. It is a bushy, spreading plant, with dense, narrow leaves and richly fragrant heads of tiny flowers that appear throughout summer and earn it the common name of sweet alyssum. The range of colour is fairly restricted. White is the most popular choice, with pink and lilac shades less commonly seen. Its liking for well-drained soil makes it a good choice for edging borders, planting between paving stones, as a summer fill-in for rockeries, or in window boxes.

**PROPAGATION** Sow seed under glass at 10-13°C/50-55 °F during late winter or early spring, prick out and harden off before planting in the flowering site in mid-spring. Seeds can also be sown direct in the flowering site during spring, with sequential sowings at six-week intervals to prolong the flowering period.

**GROWING** Alyssum thrives in neutral to alkaline soil, well drained and not too rich, in full sun.

**VARIETIES** 'Little Dorrit', compact white; 'Violet Queen', compact purple; 'Rosie O'Day *(above)*, pink; 'Wonderland', rose-carmine.

**POSSIBLE PROBLEMS** Seedlings, particularly if direct sown, may be eaten by slugs.

# TAGETES

| summer | half-hardy | full sun | 15-23cm/6-9in | 15cm/6in |

The daintiest and most elegant of the marigolds also has the most pleasantly scented foliage with a sweet, citrus smell. *T. tenuifolia*, also known as *T. signata (above)*, is a compact plant, perfect for edging or containers, with small, single flowers borne in such profusion that they almost hide the attractive, ferny foliage. Like the other types of tagetes, the flower colour is restricted to yellows and oranges, but the habit is far more refined than that of the African and French marigolds so commonly seen.

**PROPAGATION** Sow seed indoors in mid-spring at 16-18°C/60-65°F. Prick out and harden off young plants before planting out when all danger of frost is past. Seed can also be sown in the flowering position in late spring for later flowers.

**GROWING** Choose a sunny spot, with fertile and well-drained soil. Dead-heading will ensure flowers are produced all summer long.

**VARIETIES** 'Lemon Gem'; 'Paprika' a hot orangey-red; 'Golden Gem'.

**POSSIBLE PROBLEMS** Grey mould in wet weather.

---

## ▦ SPECIAL CARE TIP

*To prolong flowering, trim off dead flowerheads, water well and give a weak foliar feed. Flowering should extend overall from mid-summer to early autumn.*

## ▦ ORGANIC TIP

*There is anecdotal evidence that the smell of tagetes is a deterrent to aphids. Although this sort of thing cannot really be relied on, it is fun to experiment. Try planting 'Paprika' next to pale yellow nasturtiums, so often covered with hoards of black bean aphids, and see if it works.*

# OENOTHERA

|  |  |  |  |  |
|---|---|---|---|---|
| summer | hardy | full sun | 45cm/18in | 15cm/6in |

*Oenothera trichocalyx* is really a short-lived perennial but is usually grown as a hardy biennial. The flower colour most often associated with oenothera is yellow, but this species has white, sweetly scented flowers which appear in great quantities in early summer, but are short-lived. The common name, evening primrose, is rather deceptive since it is not a primrose and most of the perennial types flower during the day. It is an excellent plant for a sunny, mixed border.

**PROPAGATION** Sow seed in pots of ordinary seed compost, with the protection of a cold frame if possible, during mid-spring. Prick out the seedlings and grow on in a nursery bed before transplanting to the flowering position in mid-autumn.

**GROWING** Soil should be well drained, although frequent watering is needed in dry spells. Choose a sunny and open position.

**VARIETIES** *O. biennis (above)* is a 90cm/3ft yellow biennial that flowers from early summer to mid-autumn. Self-sown seedlings can be a nuisance.

**POSSIBLE PROBLEMS** Root rot in damp conditions.

# MENTZELIA

|  |  |  |  |  |
|---|---|---|---|---|
| summer | hardy | full sun | 45cm/18in | 25cm/10in |

This bushy annual is ideal for the front of a sunny border. The showy, golden-yellow flowers are held in clusters at the ends of well-branched stems with coarsely serrated leaves, and appear from early to mid-summer. In seed catalogues, it will be categorized as either *M. lindleyi* or *Bartonia aurea (above)*, and it the only species that is really worth growing.

**PROPAGATION** Sow seed thinly in the flowering site in mid- to late spring, when the soil starts to warm up. In a particularly cold spring, it can be sown in pots for planting out when conditions improve. Thin seedlings.

**GROWING** A good choice for an exposed site, *mentzelia* will tolerate both wind and heat, although humidity can cause problems. It is tolerant of alkaline soil, but free-draining conditions are essential.

**VARIETIES** There are no named varieties.

**POSSIBLE PROBLEMS** Generally trouble-free.

---

■ PLANTING TIP

*When the flowers of O. biennis finally open in the early evening, you can actually see the petals start to unfold in a series of jerky movements. Children of all ages love to watch this, so plant near a patio where you can enjoy the evening fragrance and watch the pollinating moths that are attracted.*

---

■ PLANTING TIP

*If your soil remains water-logged during summer, this annual could be grown in a raised bed or a rockery, where the free-draining conditions can be assured.*

# NICOTIANA

| summer | half-hardy | full sun | 75-90cm/2-3ft | 30cm/12in |

A must for the aromatic garden, the imposing tobacco plant has bold, slightly sticky-feeling leaves and stems, with beautifully scented trumpet-shaped flowers held in loose sprays. N. alata, which you will also find listed as N. affinis, has been hybridized to overcome the tendency of its flowers to open only in the evening, although the long flowering period, from early summer to early or mid-autumn, has been retained. Grow them to lend height to an annual or in a mixed border.

PROPAGATION Sow seeds in late winter to early spring, under glass at 18°C/64°F. The seed is tiny, so surface sow as thinly as possible. Prick out and harden off before planting out once any danger of frost is past.

GROWING A rich, well-drained soil is best, although the plants should be watered during dry spells. Staking may be needed for tall varieties if the site is exposed. Flowering can be prolonged by regular dead-heading, but as the flower spikes are suitable for cutting, this will probably not be necessary.

VARIETIES 'Sensation Mixed' gives a lovely combination of colours, including white, cream, red, pink and purple, with flowers open all day; 'Lime Green' (above), is greatly favoured by flower arrangers. A really tall species is N. sylvestris, reaching 1.5m/5ft.

POSSIBLE PROBLEMS Aphids.

# LIMNANTHES

| summer | hardy | full sun | 15cm/6in | 10cm/4in |

Limnanthes douglasii (above), the poached egg flower, has a great deal to recommend it. It is easily grown from seed and will often self sow, it attracts a variety of beneficial insects to the garden, and it makes an unusual front-of border or rockery plant. Add to this the fragrant appeal of its wide-open, yellow and white flowers, sometimes reaching 2.5cm/1in across, and attractive ferny foliage, and it really is irresistible.

PROPAGATION Simply sow seed in the flowering position in early spring for summer flowering, or in early autumn for spring flowering. Overwintering plants will form quite large clumps.

GROWING Plant in a sunny position. Hot, humid conditions are not tolerated, so try a raised area, such as a rockery. Thin seedlings and keep well weeded and watered.

VARIETIES There are no named varieties.

POSSIBLE PROBLEMS Generally trouble-free.

## ▮ PROPAGATION TIP

Sowing tiny seeds sufficiently thinly is always a problem. Try mixing the seed with some silver sand before sprinkling it on to moist compost. This will also make it easier to see where you have already sown, particularly if the seed is dark in colour, as is the case with nicotiana seeds.

## ▮ ORGANIC TIP

One of the characteristics that makes limnanthes so attractive to hoverflies is its open, simple flower shape that gives the insects easy access to the nectar they feed on. Flowers that have been bred to form doubles are not nearly so appealing and so are less valuable for an organic gardener.

# CHEIRANTHUS

| spring | hardy | full sun | 22-60cm/9in-2ft | 20-30cm/8-12in |
|---|---|---|---|---|

Wallflowers are one of the mainstays of spring bedding schemes, along with tulips, forget-me-nots and primulas. Their warm, clove-like fragrance makes these biennials a valuable addition to the aromatic garden, despite the fact that the seed for the following year's plants has to be sown just as the current year's plants are starting to fade. Many gardeners forget, in the rush of spring jobs, and buy bare-rooted planted in autumn.

**PROPAGATION** Sow seed of *Cheiranthus cheiri* outside in a nursery bed in early summer. Pinch out the tips to encourage bushiness, then transplant to their flowering positions in autumn. In very cold winters, the plants can be grown in frames.

**GROWING** Well-drained, alkaline soil is best for wallflowers. Choose a sunny site, although a little shade during the morning or afternoon is acceptable. In a frosty area, plant out in a sheltered spot.

**VARIETIES** Mixed or single colours are available. For dwarf plants, choose 'Orange Bedder' *(above)*, 'Primrose Bedder', or 'Tom Thumb Mixed'. For tall plants, try 'Blood Red', 'Ivory White', or 'Cloth of Gold', a golden-yellow.

**POSSIBLE PROBLEMS** Club root.

## ORGANIC TIP

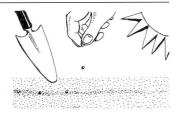

*If you grow brassicas in your vegetable plot, raise your own wallflowers from seed, rather than run the risk of bringing in club root on bought plants.*

# DIANTHUS

| summer | hardy | full sun | 30-60cm/12in-2ft | 20-25cm/8-10in |
|---|---|---|---|---|

The dianthus family is a large and varied one. *D. barbatus* is the sweet william, usually grown as a biennial for early summer flowering. It has an old-fashioned look, and is more at home in a perennial border or cottage garden than in a formal bedding scheme. Its densely packed, flattened heads of spice-scented flowers in shades of red, pink and white are often bi-coloured, and are held on stiff, upright, bright green stems.

**PROPAGATION** Sow in a nursery bed outdoors in early summer for flowering the following summer. They should be transplanted to their flowering positions in autumn. Some varieties can be grown as annuals. Sow under glass in early spring at 13°C/55°F, harden off and plant out in late spring.

**GROWING** Sweet williams perform best in a sunny position, in ordinary, well-drained soil. Acid soils would benefit from a dressing of lime. They should not need staking unless the site is very windy.

**VARIETIES** 'Dunnets Dark Crimson', an old, single-colour variety; 'Indian Carpet Mixed' *(above)* is suitable for growing as an annual. *D. superbus* is another biennial, grown in the same way, but more like a garden pink in habit. Suitable for rock gardens or herbaceous borders, they tolerate more shade than most other species.

**POSSIBLE PROBLEMS** Rust.

## SPECIAL CARE TIP

*D. barbatus is actually a short-lived perennial. By cutting it back hard after flowering, usually with shears, it can be encouraged to flower satisfactorily for another year or two, although there will inevitably be some reduction in the quality of the blooms if they are grown for much longer.*

# MALCOLMIA

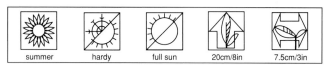

| summer | hardy | full sun | 20cm/8in | 7.5cm/3in |

One of the simplest, fastest-growing annuals, Virginia stock or *M. maritima (above)* is a great favourite for children's gardens. Open, four-petalled, fragrant flowers in white, pink, mauve or creamy-yellow appear on thin stems just four weeks after sowing. They will even tolerate partial shade. This paragon is sometimes ignored because of its very simplicity, but a pinch of seed between paving stones, at the edge of borders or in containers will delight all who see the result.

**PROPAGATION** Make successive sowings in ordinary garden soil. Sow in spring for summer flowers, in summer for late summer flowers, and in autumn for spring flowers.

**GROWING** Although they do very well with no further attention, thinning seedlings will result in more compact plants.

**VARIETIES** Mixed colours are most common, but single selections are available such as 'Crimson King'.

**POSSIBLE PROBLEMS** Generally trouble-free.

# ASPERULA

| summer | hardy | semi-shade | 30cm/12in | 10cm/4in |

*Asperula orientalis* syn. *A. azurea* syn. *A. setosa* (above), comes from a large family of mostly small annuals and perennials. The scented, pale blue flowers of this hardy annual appear in mid-summer. They are held in clusters at the end of slender stems bearing slightly hairy, mid-green leaves, and are suitable for cutting. They are unusual for annuals, in that they thrive in partial shade, and are suitable for planting under roses or between shrubs.

**PROPAGATION** Sow in their flowering site in mid-spring for flowering in mid-summer.

**GROWING** Select a site with moisture retentive soil and in partial shade for this annual asperula. Water well while the plants are becoming established.

**VARIETIES** There are no named varieties.

**POSSIBLE PROBLEMS** Generally trouble-free.

---

### ▪ PLANTING TIP

*Try mixing together the seeds of Virginia stock with those of night-scented stock for sowing together. The former have showy flowers but are not especially fragrant at night. The latter have rather insignificant flowers but the scent is exquisite. Together, they make a winning combination.*

### ▪ SPECIAL CARE TIP

*Asperula can be grown on in pots under glass to provide a scented indoor display of flowers for mid-spring. Lift spring-sown plants from the garden in autumn, pinch out and pot up in clumps using an all-purpose compost. Maintain a minimum temperature of 4°C/40°F. Discard after the display is over.*

# ECHIUM

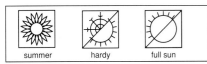

| | | | | |
|---|---|---|---|---|
| summer | hardy | full sun | 90cm/3ft | 45cm/18in |

There are both biennial and half-hardy types of echiums, but *E. plantagineum* syn. *E. lycopsis*, is a showy annual suitable for a mixed border or among other annuals. Mixed-colour seed packets will give a range of white, pink, red, purple or blue bell-shaped flowers in long-lasting spikes 25cm/10in long. The stems are rather stiff with narrow, hairy leaves. The fragrant flowers appear from mid-summer to late autumn, and are very attractive to bees.

**PROPAGATION** Sow seeds where they are to flower, in autumn for earlier flowering, or in mid-spring in colder areas. Thin seedlings to the correct spacing.

**GROWING** Ordinary, well-drained garden soil is suitable, but a light or medium texture gives the very best results. Sow in full sun.

**VARIETIES** For front of borders or in a windy site, try 'Dwarf Hybrids' *(above)* or 'Blue Bedder'.

**POSSIBLE PROBLEMS** Generally trouble-free.

# PHACELIA

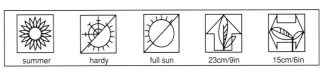

| | | | | |
|---|---|---|---|---|
| summer | hardy | full sun | 23cm/9in | 15cm/6in |

A blue as bright and intense as the flowers of *P. campanularia (above)* is a rarity in the garden, and certainly among annuals. This fast-growing, hardy annual, sometimes called the California bluebell, has spreading stems with oval, toothed leaves that are aromatic when crushed gently. The bell-shaped flowers turn upwards to reveal a paler centre and bright yellow stamens, making it irresistible to bees as well as gardeners.

**PROPAGATION** Seed is the only method of propagation. Sow in the flowering site in spring, or in autumn in areas with mild winters. Protection with a cloche may be necessary in this case, as the young plants grow rapidly.

**GROWING** Flowers are produced all summer long provided it is not too hot. Ordinary, well-drained soil is suitable, but results are better if it is light and not too richly nourished. A little shade is tolerated.

**VARIETIES** 'Blue Bonnet' grows approximately twice as tall.

**POSSIBLE PROBLEMS** Generally trouble-free.

## ORGANIC TIP

*As well as attracting bees, echium will encourage other beneficial insects into your garden to deal with the troublesome ones, particularly aphids.*

## PLANTING TIP

*For a striking effect, sow* phacelia *next to golden* mentzelia *in an annual border or, for a softer combination, sow them with pink and white* malcolmia.

# CLEOME

|  |  |  |  |  |
|---|---|---|---|---|
| summer | half-hardy | full sun | 1.2m/4ft | 45cm/18in |

Despite its exotic appearance, C. *spinosa (above)*, commonly known as the spider flower, will continue flowering from mid-summer until the first frosts. It makes an imposing, bushy specimen feature in the middle of a flower bed, but is equally at home filling in the spaces in an immature shrub border or grown in a container. The aromatic, fingered leaves are a good foil for the sprays of mostly pink and white flowers with their projecting stamens.

**PROPAGATION** Sow seed under glass in early to mid-spring, at about 18°C/65°F. Harden off young plants carefully, pricking them out and growing them on in pots until all danger of frost is past and the soil is warming up.

**GROWING** Plant out in fertile, well-drained soil, preferably in full sun or very light shade. Shelter from strong winds is highly recommended.

**VARIETIES** The colour range is fairly limited, but choose from 'Colour Fountain Mixed', with pink, rose, lilac, purple and white flowers, or single shades such as the white 'Helen Campbell', or the carmine 'Cherry Queen'.

**POSSIBLE PROBLEMS** Greenfly on young shoots.

# MATTHIOLA

|  |  |  |  |  |
|---|---|---|---|---|
| summer | hardy | full sun | 30-75cm/12in-2½ft | 15-20cm/6-8in |

The fragrant bedding stocks derived from M. *incana* form upright spikes of single or double flowers in shades of pink, purple, red, white and yellow, set off by the greyish foliage. There are a number of groups that are propagated in different ways. Ten Week stocks, Perpetual Flowering stocks, Trysomic stocks and Selectable Double strains are all grown as annuals. Brompton stocks are biennials and flower in spring. The East Lothian or Intermediate stocks can be treated as either annuals or biennials. All make excellent cut flowers.

**PROPAGATION** Summer flowering annuals should be sown under glass in early spring, then pricked out and hardened off before planting out. Alternatively, they can be sown in their flowering position in mid-spring. Biennials are sown in nursery beds in summer, moved to their final positions in autumn and flower the following spring.

**GROWING** Well-drained soil is best, and even very alkaline conditions are tolerated. Full sun, with very light shade in hot conditions, gives good results, but high humidity increases the spread of disease.

**VARIETIES** M. *bicornis* – the night-scented stock, is an easy, fast-growing annual worth sowing near a front door as is 'Giant Perfection Mixed' *(above)*.

**POSSIBLE PROBLEMS** Flea beetle; aphids.

**■ ORGANIC TIP**

*Natural predators of the aphid, can be encouraged into your garden if you stop using chemical sprays. Hoverfly larvae can eat aphids at the rate of one a minute. Limnanthes douglasii, the poached egg plant (see page 44), attracts hoverflies, and it makes sense to sow them near vulnerable specimens.*

**■ SPECIAL CARE TIP**

*Double Trysomic stocks are most popular, but all seed packets contain a mixture of single and double. You can distinguish seedlings by their colour. Double plants have more yellow seedlings, while singles are darker green. If there is no difference, reduce the temperature slightly and it will become clear.*

# PETUNIA

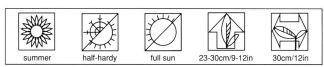

| | | | | |
|---|---|---|---|---|
| summer | half-hardy | full sun | 23-30cm/9-12in | 30cm/12in |

Petunias have been hybridized almost beyond recognition to give the large-flowered, bushy, colourful plants so popular as summer bedding. Doubles, frilled petals, stripes and veining are all variations on the soft, funnel-shaped flowers in shades of red, purple, blue, pink, yellow and white, that are borne in profusion above sticky, pale green stems and leaves. For the best vanilla scent, choose single flowers in shades of blue and purple, and plant in window boxes, hanging baskets, containers or as edging for the most striking results.

**PROPAGATION** Sow seed under glass in mid-spring, at 16-21°C/60-70°F. Prick out into pots and harden off before planting out after danger of frost is past.

**GROWING** A fertile soil, enriched before planting if very light or poor, is ideal. Full sun is preferred, but a little shade is tolerated. Dead-head regularly, and cut stems back if they become too straggly.

**VARIETIES** Resisto hybrids stand up to rain better than most. 'Blue Joy' violet-blue; 'Brass Band', cream; 'Resisto Mixed' *(above)*; 'White Joy'.

**POSSIBLE PROBLEMS** Aphids; virus.

# LATHYRUS

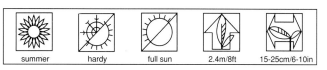

| | | | | |
|---|---|---|---|---|
| summer | hardy | full sun | 2.4m/8ft | 15-25cm/6-10in |

Popular, pretty and easily grown from seed, the sweet pea, *L. odoratus (above)*, is a fragrant climber no garden should be without. The original species, a native of southern Italy, has been intensively bred for reliability, height, colour, cutting and fragrance to give a vast choice of varieties; there are even dwarf varieties. All share the characteristic pea-shaped flower with large wing petals and a central keel carried on long stems.

**PROPAGATION** Sow seeds in pots under glass in autumn or early spring. Pinch out to encourage bushiness when the seedlings are 10cm/4in high. Harden off and plant out. Alternatively sow in their flowering position in autumn or spring. Autumn sowings may need protection with a cloche.

**GROWING** Deeply cultivated, slightly alkaline soil to which plenty of well-rotted organic matter has been added gives best results. Sweet peas like their heads in the sun but their roots should be shaded. Provide support for climbing varieties.

**VARIETIES** Spencer varieties include 'Leamington', deep lavender; 'Winston Churchill, bright crimson; 'Mrs R Bolton', almond-pink; 'Hunter's Moon', creamy-primrose; 'Royal Wedding', pure white. For dwarf plants in mixed colours, choose 'Little Sweetheart' or 'Snoopea'.

**POSSIBLE PROBLEMS** Slugs; aphids; damping-off of seedlings.

## ▨ SPECIAL CARE TIP

*Although petunias need a fertile soil, too rich a soil, too much moisture and shade will encourage the production of foliage instead of flowers.*

## ▨ PROPAGATION TIP

*Sweet pea seeds can be slow to germinate, because their thick seed coats keep out water. By soaking them for 12 hours before sowing, this problem can be greatly reduced. Another method is to nick the seed coat with a knife, but damage can easily be caused, either to the seed or, more often, to the gardener's fingers.*

## SCABIOSA

| summer | hardy | full sun | 90cm/3ft | 23cm/9in |

The shape of the round, densely packed flowerheads, with tiny projecting stamens give *S. atropurpurea* its common name of pincushion. In shades of blue, purple, mauve, red, pink and white, they are sweetly scented and excellent for cutting, as they are produced all summer on long, wiry stems.

**PROPAGATION** Sow seed in the flowering site in spring or autumn, with protection over winter if necessary. In cold areas, seed can be sown under glass in early spring, but should be hardened off before planting out.

**GROWING** Ordinary, well-drained soil in full sun is suitable, and alkaline conditions are tolerated quite happily. Tall types should be given some support while the plants are still small. Dead-head regularly.

**VARIETIES** 'Cockade Mixed' is a popular variety. For single colours, try 'Blue Moon' or 'Rose Cockade' *(above)*. 'Tom Thumb' is a dwarf type.

**POSSIBLE PROBLEMS** Slugs; snails.

## MIRABILIS

| summer | half-hardy | full sun | 60-90cm/2-3ft | 30cm/12in |

The common name marvel of Peru gives a clue to the origins of this fascinating plant, while its other name, the four o'clock plant, indicates something about its habits. In hot weather, the strongly scented flowers open only in the afternoon and evening, although cooler conditions will induce them to open earlier in the day. The funnel-shaped flowers appear in a range of colours, including red, pink, white and pink studded, among dark to mid-green leaves on a bushy, spreading plant.

**PROPAGATION** The usual method of propagation is by seed sown indoors during late winter or early spring at 18°C/64°F. Prick out seedlings and harden off carefully before planting outside.

**GROWING** A sheltered site in full sun is essential. Water in dry conditions.

**VARIETIES** Single colour selections are sometimes available such as *M. jalapa (above)*, which has pink flowers. 'Pygmea' is a compact form, suitable for container growing.

**POSSIBLE PROBLEMS** Generally trouble-free.

### ▓ SPECIAL CARE TIP

Many tall annuals benefit from support, provided before they need it. The recommended pea sticks are branched twigs, often garden prunings, stuck into the ground to form a framework that will eventually be covered by the growing plants. Of course, diseased prunings should not be used.

### ▓ PROPAGATION TIP

*M. jalapa is usually raised yearly from seed, but it forms tubers that can be overwintered, provided they are lifted before the first frost.*

# HELIOTROPIUM

summer / half-hardy / full sun / 45cm/18in / 30cm/12in

It would be fun to try out the scent of *H. × hybridum (above)* on unsuspecting friends to see if they guess the common name, cherry pie. For sunny, sheltered gardens *heliotropium* makes an unusual addition to bedding schemes and is an excellent choice for containers. Each flower is tiny, but the clusters are dense and freely produced, mostly in shades of purple and blue, above dark green, wrinkled leaves.

**PROPAGATION** Sow seeds indoors during late winter at about 16-18°C/61-64°F, prick out and harden off before planting out once all danger of frost is past.

**GROWING** Plant in full sun, in a sheltered position in well-drained but fertile soil. Pinch out the tips of young plants to make a bushy shape. Dead-head regularly.

**VARIETIES** 'Royal Marine' is a deep violet-blue. There are few other varieties available.

**POSSIBLE PROBLEMS** Generally trouble-free.

# PERILLA

summer / half-hardy / full sun / 60cm/2ft / 30cm/12in

Although *P. frutescens (above)* produces spikes of tiny white flowers, they are best pinched out as soon as they appear. This useful plant is grown for its dark purple, glistening, deeply veined leaves, which release a warm, spicy fragrance when crushed. The bushy shape makes perilla an excellent dot plant in formal bedding schemes, where it acts as a foil for brightly coloured flowers.

**PROPAGATION** Sow seed inside from early to mid-spring at about 18°C/65°F. Prick out seedings into pots and harden off carefully, only planting out once any danger of frost is past.

**GROWING** Plant in full sun, in a sheltered position. Any ordinary, fertile soil is suitable, but feeding will produce larger plants.

**VARIETIES** 'Folliis Atropurpurea Laciniata' has attractive crumpled-looking leaves.

**POSSIBLE PROBLEMS** Generally trouble-free.

## SPECIAL CARE TIP

Heliotropium *is really an evergreen shrub and can be overwintered under glass. Try growing it as a standard. Use a rooted cutting in a pot. Do not pinch out, but remove side shoots and train the stem up a cane. When it is tall enough, pinch out the tip leaving four sets of leaves to form the head.*

## SPECIAL CARE TIP

*Apart from improving the appearance, it is better to remove the insignificant flower spikes to prevent the spread of self-sown seedlings.*

51

# BULBS, CORMS AND RHIZOMES

**The time of year most people associate with bulbs is the early spring, and there are certainly spectacular effects to be created with bulbs then. All the more so, because little else is in flower. But virtually a whole year of flowers can be achieved from bulbs, corms and rhizomes.**

The difference between bulbs, corms and rhizomes is a botanical one. In each case, the dormant body is a storage organ. In the case of bulbs, it has developed from modified leaf bases, corms are modified stem bases and rhizomes are underground stems. The term 'bulb' is commonly, but not quite accurately, used for all three types. What they do have in common is that, during the plant's dormant season they provide a storage body, from which the new shoot will emerge. It helps to understand this, because it influences the aftercare of bulbs, which is often neglected, but is very important if the plants are to perform well in subsequent years. There is a huge choice of colours, sizes, habits and scents — bulbous plants are among some of the most highly scented — and they earn their place in every garden.

**CHOOSING AND PLANTING BULBS**  Bulbs can last for many years, and may even increase when treated well and planted in a suitable position, so it is very important to choose good quality, healthy specimens in the first place. They are usually sold in the dormant season, although some genera, particularly snowdrops and hardy cyclamen, will transplant better in the green, straight after flowering. Spring-flowering bulbs appear for sale in autumn, while summer- and autumn-flowering types can be bought in spring.

A lot can be told about a bulb just by its appearance. The larger the bulb, the more likely it is to produce a flower in the first season after planting, but the more expensive, too. Immature bulbs are a cost-saving buy provided you are prepared to wait a couple of years for flowers. Any bulbs you choose should be firm to the touch. Avoid any that are soft and shrivelled, dented, damaged or obviously diseased-looking. A long pale shoot is a bad sign, but a thick, fresh green growth bud, just emerging from the bulb is fine, provided you can plant soon. For the widest choice, select bulbs from a specialist mail-order catalogue. Whoever you buy from, try and make sure that the bulbs were raised in cultivation, and not lifted from the wild, where they are becoming increasingly rare.

Most bulbs will thrive in a soil that is both well drained and moisture retentive. A poor, thin soil can be coaxed towards this ideal condition by the addition of some well-rotted organic matter, and adding sharp grit will improve soil that is heavy and slow to drain. Prior to planting it is a good idea to add bone meal or a special bulb fertilizer as a base dressing. It is important to plant bulbs at the correct depth, otherwise they may fail to flower altogether. Although there are exceptions, most bulbs should be planted in a hole three times their height. For example, a bulb that measures 5cm/2in from top to bottom should be planted in a hole 15cm/6in deep, and covered by 10cm/4in of soil.

To allow the roots to develop healthily, make sure that the base of the bulb is in contact with the soil underneath, not dangling in an air pocket. Finally, label your bulbs carefully, and even mix some silver sand with the soil you replace on top, so that you won't make the awful mistake of plunging your border fork into the ground and spearing bulbs you had forgotten about.

Half-hardy bulbs are treated in much the same way, but are not planted out until the danger of a hard frost is past. After flowering the foliage should be allowed to dry out, then the bulbs lifted before the first frost of autumn. They can be stored in dry, frost-free conditions, then cleaned and replanted the following year.

The aftercare of hardy bulbs is very important for their continuing vigour. Foliage should be allowed to die down naturally, not hacked off prematurely, or tied into tight twists. It does look untidy, but careful planting will ensure that something else attracts the eye away from the leaves which can then be left to fulfil their role of making food that will be stored in the bulb for the following year. This is important for bulbs that are naturalized in grassland and lawns, too. Lovely effects can be produced with fritillaries, daffodils, snowdrops or grape hyacinths, but it can be a hard life for a bulb. They have enough competition for water and food from the surrounding grass without being cut down in their prime. Make sure you only naturalize bulbs in an area of grass you can leave without cutting until the foliage dies down naturally, in mid- to late summer. For spring-flowering bulbs in any position, a liquid feed or a top-dressing of a balanced fertilizer applied after flowering will give a boost to the bulb and ensure good flowering and, possibly, an increase in your stock in years to come. Established summer- and autumn-flowering bulbs should be fed at the same time, in early- to mid-spring.

Another common practice is to grow specially treated spring bulbs, usually hyacinths and narcissi, in pots for flowering indoors during winter, using a method called forcing. This involves planting the bulbs, watering, then storing in cold, dark conditions for several weeks, during which time the roots will develop. They are then brought into light but still cool conditions for the shoot to develop to flowering point. These bulbs are more expensive than the untreated kind, and the treatment depletes their vigour so they may not flower again for several years. There is no need to discard them, though. They will eventually recover, particularly if planted out in a spare part of the garden where they can recover their strength, and treated to a feed during the growing season, but in future years they will flower at the normal time.

**BULBS IN THE GARDEN** The earliest spring bulbs are small plants, and for maximum impact both visually and in terms of their scent, they must be positioned with care. In raised beds or in containers, near to the house and beside paths, they give pleasure to everyone that passes. Early bulbs can be planted under deciduous shrubs and trees to make the most of the light that filters through the bare branches. Later on, little or nothing will thrive there, but groups of snowdrops, aconites, crocus, early daffodils, cyclamen or dwarf iris will make an unforgettable picture, especially if planted in blocks of single colour.

From spring on, the garden can be filled with an almost constant succession of scents and colours, with hyacinths, which make a wonderful window box or container feature, daffodils which combine beautifully with pansies or polyanthus in borders and containers, then tulips, classically combined with forget-me-nots or wallflowers for exquisite fragrance that carries over long distances.

Summer bulbs have far more competition from other plants, so it is just as well that they include some of the most spectacular flowers and perfumes in the garden. Lilies have bold flowers of great beauty, as well as wonderful heavy perfume, and they work well in a variety of border styles from cottage-inspired to formal, modern plantings.

Summer- and autumn-flowering bulbs lend grandeur to mixed borders, but are also very suitable for container growing, and a pot of lilies or acidanthera can be moved near the house as their fragrant flowers come into bloom, then placed in shelter as it gets colder. Even in the depths of winter, *Iris unguicularis* can be depended on to produce its short-stemmed, lavender-blue flowers in sharply-drained, sunny, sheltered borders, a welcome and strangely exotic sight at that time of year, and an excellent cut flower with a scent of violets. From then on, the more traditional spring bulbs take over once again.

## GALTONIA

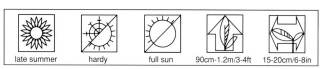

| late summer | hardy | full sun | 90cm-1.2m/3-4ft | 15-20cm/6-8in |

A spectacular and unusual bulb for summer borders is *G. candicans (above)*, sometimes called the summer hyacinth. Greenish-white, bell-like flowers hang from loosely-packed flower spikes that rise above strap-shaped leaves, and bring a fresh look to the garden in late summer. They make excellent cut flowers, and the scent is more noticeable once they are brought indoors.

**PROPAGATION** The bulbs produce offsets that can be planted out in a nursery bed to reach flowering size. Seed is not always produced, but should be sown under glass in spring. Flowering size will not be reached for several years.

**GROWING** Plant bulbs in spring at a depth of 15-20cm/6-8in and 30cm/12in apart. Choose a sunny position, with shelter and a well-drained soil rich in organic matter. In cold areas the bulbs may need to be protected in winter.

**VARIETIES** There are no other garden varieties.

**POSSIBLE PROBLEMS** Generally trouble-free in the right conditions.

## GALANTHUS

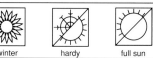 

| winter | hardy | full sun | 15-25cm/6-10in | 10-20cm/4-8in |

A welcome sight on cold winter days, snowdrops have a fresh, dainty look that amply rewards the effort of finding the right position for them. Their scent is probably best appreciated once they have been cut and brought indoors, where the honeyed-primrose scent is more likely to reach nose-level, but it does seem a shame. There are a number of distinct species and varieties, but to the non-expert eye they are difficult to tell apart. All have nodding white flowers and healthy-looking, strap-shaped leaves.

**PROPAGATION** Clumps may self seed, otherwise sow collected or bought seed in pots and grow on in shade with plenty of moisture. Division is the more common method, with congested clumps being split and replanted straight after flowering.

**GROWING** Plant bulbs 8cm/3in apart and 10cm/4in deep in moist soil in partial shade. They can be used as underplanting for deciduous shrubs or trees.

**VARIETIES** *G. nivalis (above)* is native to Europe and lightly scented of primrose; *G. elwesii* is about twice as tall. 'Magnet' and 'Straffan' are honey scented. 'Atkinsii' is a vigorous, slightly taller type.

**POSSIBLE PROBLEMS** Sometimes difficult to establish.

### ▓ PROPAGATION TIP

*Galtonia dislikes disturbance, so plant it in a location where you will not be cultivating regularly, between shrubs in a mixed border, for example. If removing offsets for propagation, make sure you do so in the dormant season, and replant immediately so as to cause least shock to the plant.*

### ▓ PLANTING TIP

*Buying dry bulbs of snowdrops can be risky. At best, only a proportion will grow and at worst, none at all. Buy them just after flowering when you can see the foliage is still fresh looking, at the stage called 'in the green', or better still ask a friend to lift and divide an established clump for you.*

## LEUCOJUM

| | | | | |
|---|---|---|---|---|
| late winter | hardy | semi-shade | 15-20cm/6-8in | 10cm/4in |

*Leucojum vernum (above)*, the spring snowflake, is rather similar to the snowdrop in appearance, but the fragrant blooms are generally larger and have a green dot at the end of each petal. It is a strong, easily pleased bulb suitable for naturalizing in grass or growing in moist and shady areas. It even grows well on a heavy clay soil.

**PROPAGATION** Division of overcrowded clumps is the simplest method of propogation, as offsets are freely produced in good conditions. Plants raised from seed take several years to reach flowering size.

**GROWING** Snowflakes are less difficult to establish than snowdrops, and can be successfully established from dry bulbs planted in autumn about 10cm/4in deep.

**VARIETIES** 'Carpathicum' varies only in that it has yellow dots on the petals.

**POSSIBLE PROBLEMS** Generally trouble-free.

## CONVALLARIA

| | | | | |
|---|---|---|---|---|
| late spring | hardy | semi-shade | 15-23cm/6-9in | 60cm/2ft |

For all its small size, *C. majalis (above)* or lily-of-the-valley has a powerful and beautiful scent. The fresh green leaves will spread to provide ground cover if the situation is right, and the arching flower stems of waxy-white nodding bells are a delight whether cut for posy arrangements or left where they are. An ideal position would be the dappled shade beneath deciduous shrubs, where it would provide interest early in the season.

**PROPAGATION** The spreading rhizomes produce upright buds on the crown, commonly called pips. Clumps should be divided in autumn and replanted with the pips 8-10cm/3-4in apart, and just below the surface of the soil. From seed, plants take at least three years to reach flowering size.

**GROWING** Plant in partial shade, in moisture-retentive soil enriched with plenty of leaf mould, or other organic matter. Mulch in summer after the leaves have died down.

**VARIETIES** 'Fortin's Giant' has larger flowers; 'Rosea' produces pink flowers.

**POSSIBLE PROBLEMS** Generally trouble-free.

### ▦ PLANTING TIP

*Leucojum's tolerance of different sites makes it a perfect choice for brightening up rock gardens in winter when there may be little other interest.*

### ▦ SPECIAL CARE TIP

*For forcing indoor flowers in winter, plant mature pips in pots in a well-drained but rich compost. Keep cold but frost free mid-winter, then bring into room temperature and water regularly. Crowns specially prepared for forcing can be bought, and will give better results than home produced.*

## CRINUM

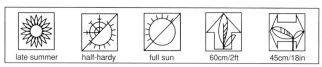

| late summer | half-hardy | full sun | 60cm/2ft | 45cm/18in |

The beautifully shaped and fragrant rose-pink flowers of
C. × *powellii* amply reward the care it needs for success. The
base of a sunny wall will provide the shelter and heat that
crinums love, but do not neglect watering. The leaves are long,
rather sprawling and evergreen, but at least absent-minded
gardeners will not forget where the bulbs are planted.

**PROPAGATION** Remove offsets in spring, pot on and grow
on in shelter for a couple of years. Take care when removing –
crinums dislike disturbance. Plants grown from seed will take
up to five years to flower.

**GROWING** If the required conditions cannot be provided,
give up and grow the bulbs in pots under glass, moving them
outside during summer. Winter protection for the crowns of
plants grown outside, as for amaryllis *(see page 62)*, will help.
The bulbs must be planted deeply – at about 25cm/10in.

**VARIETIES** 'Album' *(above)* has white flowers; 'Krelagai' is
deep pink.

**POSSIBLE PROBLEMS** Generally trouble-free.

## CARDIOCRINUM

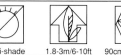

| summer | hardy | semi-shade | 1.8-3m/6-10ft | 90cm-1.2m/3-4ft |

Definitely not a plant for a small garden, the giant Himalayan
lily, C. *giganteum (above)*, is a truly spectacular sight, with its
white trumpet-shaped flowers with purple markings at the
throat, sometimes borne 20 to the stem. The fragrance is
splendid and the heart-shaped, shiny leaves provide additional
interest slightly closer to the ground.

**PROPAGATION** After the effort of producing such a
spectacular flower, the bulbs die. Offsets can be removed in
autumn and will reach flowering size in up to five years.
Otherwise, sow seed when ripe, providing some shelter. They
will take around seven years to flower. Most gardeners buy
new bulbs each year.

**GROWING** A rich, slightly acid and moisture retentive soil is
preferred, with some shelter. The bulbs should be planted with
the tops just below the surface of the soil.

**VARIETIES** C. *cordatum* is shorter growing, reaching a mere
1.8m/6ft, but is less hardy.

**POSSIBLE PROBLEMS** Generally trouble-free.

■ PLANTING TIP

*An alternative to growing
in front of a wall is to grow
crinum on the sunny side of
a hedge. With the right
foliage colour, this can be
a highly decorative effect,
perhaps with dark ever-
green foliage to make the
contrast more dramatic. Do
not neglect watering and
feeding as the hedge also
makes demands on the soil.*

■ PLANTING TIP

*It is possible to have
cardiocrinums each year
by buying the bulbs all in
one go, but in different
sizes. The smaller take over
from the larger as the years
pass, then, when the
smallest ones planted
have flowered and died,
the offsets of the largest
bulbs are likely to have
reached flowering size.*

# PANCRATIUM

|  |  |  |  |  |
|---|---|---|---|---|
| summer | half-hardy | full sun | 45cm/18in | 23cm/9in |

This unusual bulb needs a warm, sheltered spot in full sun if it is to produce its fragrant, star-shaped white flowers, with prominent tufted stamens. The grey-green leaves are strap-like and produced in a cluster around the flower stem, which is leafless. There may be as many as 12 flowers to each head. *P. illyricum* is the most likely species to flower in cultivation.

**PROPAGATION** Seed should be sown indoors during spring, at 16-18°C/61-64°F, but will take up to five years to produce flowers. The bulbs produce offsets that can be removed and planted in late summer.

**GROWING** Planting the bulbs deeply, with some 20cm/8in of soil on top, will improve survival over winter. Additional protection may be needed in cold areas.

**VARIETIES** *P. maritimum (above)* is slightly shorter, but produces fewer flowers.

**POSSIBLE PROBLEMS** Generally trouble-free.

# NARCISSUS (EARLY)

|  |  |  |  |  |
|---|---|---|---|---|
| early spring | hardy | full sun | 15-45cm/6-18in | 15-20cm/6-8in |

For an early show, choose narcissi or daffodils of the Tazetta or Triandrus group. The former have several flowers on each stem and are very fragrant, although some varieties are rather tender and best for growing indoors in temperate climates. In mild areas they may flower outside in winter. The latter also have several flowers per stem, but of a more drooping character and with backwards-swept outer petals. Some varieties flower rather later in the season.

**PROPAGATION** Lift and divide crowded clumps in late summer. Remove offsets which will reach flowering size in a few years. Named varieties will not come true from seed.

**GROWING** Because of the risk of cold weather early in the season, plant in a sheltered spot. Tazetta types need more sun than most *narcissi*, and will do well in a light soil. Both types are excellent pot plants.

**VARIETIES** Tazetta types include 'Soleil d'Or', yellow, and 'Paper White' *(above)*. Triandrus types include 'Liberty', yellow, and 'Thalia', white.

**POSSIBLE PROBLEMS** Stem and bulb eelworm.

## ▨ SPECIAL CARE TIP

*If the conditions are unsuitable, pancratium can be grown quite well in a frost-free greenhouse. They should be repotted every 2 or 3 years.*

## ▨ SPECIAL CARE TIP

*If daffodils are allowed to become overcrowded, they may fail to flower. This 'blindness' can be cured by lifting, dividing and feeding every few years.*

## SMILACENA

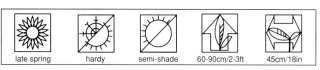

| | | | | |
|---|---|---|---|---|
| late spring | hardy | semi-shade | 60-90cm/2-3ft | 45cm/18in |

An elegant choice for woodland planting, *S. racemosa (above)* forms graceful, arching stems of pale green leaves, terminating in fluffy plumes of scented flowers that start off a greenish-white and age to a creamy shade. The broad leaves provide a dense ground cover, enhanced by the gradual spread of the rhizomatous roots, provided the conditions are suitable.

**PROPAGATION** Propagate by lifting and dividing rhizomes every few years in mid-autumn.

**GROWING** A deep, moist acid soil, enriched with leaf-mould and partially shaded is perfect for this plant. Cut back in late autumn.

**VARIETIES** *S. stellata* is a smaller plant with star-shaped flowers.

**POSSIBLE PROBLEMS** Generally trouble-free.

## LILIUM

| | | | | |
|---|---|---|---|---|
| summer | full sun | hardy | 1.2-1.8m/4-5ft | 23-30cm/9-12in |

Despite their exotic appearance, there are plenty of lilies that are easy to grow and that produce wonderful, fragrant flowers in summer. Some look best in a herbaceous or mixed border. The larger-flowered types seem more suited for growing in containers. The flower forms vary from the wide-open, bowl shaped, the narrower trumpet shaped, to the turk's cap shape in which the petals curl right back on themselves. The colour range includes pure white, pinks, oranges and yellows.

**PROPAGATION** Some lilies form clumps of bulbs that can be divided. Seeds of species will come true, but named varieties will not.

**GROWING** Plant as soon as bulbs are available, preferably in autumn. If the soil is poorly drained, dig some coarse sand into the base of the planting hole. Planting depth for most varieties is about 15cm/6in, but for *L. candidum* it is only 5cm/2in. A sunny, sheltered site is best.

**VARIETIES** *L. regale* is one of the easiest to grow and very fragrant; *L. auratum (above)* has huge flowers and look best in a pot; *L. candidum*, the madonna lily, is best left undisturbed.

**POSSIBLE PROBLEMS** *L. candidum* is prone to botrytis, a fungus disease.

---

■ PLANTING TIP

*The foliage of smilacena turns golden-yellow in autumn, even after the first frosts, so plant it in a location where this feature can be appreciated.*

■ PROPAGATION TIP

*Another method is to dig down carefully into the soil while the bulbs are dormant, and gently remove sound scales. These are inserted, base down, to half their depth in trays of compost. With a little base heat, they produce tiny bulbs within six weeks. Pot on and grow to flowering size.*

BULBS, CORMS AND RHIZOMES

## LYSICHITUM

| spring | hardy | full sun | 30-90cm/1-3ft | 45-60cm/18in-2ft |
|---|---|---|---|---|

This exotic looking plant thrives in damp or even wet soils – unusual for rhizomatous plants, so many of which need hot, well-drained conditions. The large, waxy white flowers have a single spathe, reminiscent of arum lilies, and are produced in spring before the large leaves, substantially taller than the flowers. *L. camtschatcense (above)* is the species to choose for fragrance. It is suitable for poolside or bog planting, but not for planting in water.

**PROPAGATION** Sow seed when ripe in very moist compost and grow on for a couple of years before planting out. Established plants can be divided by lifting and splitting the rhizomes.

**GROWING** Plant out between mid-spring and early summer, with as little root disturbance as possible. A deep, cool, moist root run, either in sun or light shade is best.

**VARIETIES** *L. americanus* is larger with a yellow spathe, and can be planted in shallow water.

**POSSIBLE PROBLEMS** Generally trouble-free.

## NARCISSUS (LATE)

| mid-spring | hardy | full sun | 20-42cm/8-17in | 15-20cm/6-8in |
|---|---|---|---|---|

The season of flowering can be extended by planting later forms of narcissus. Jonquilla types have a strong, spicy fragrance and should be given shelter. *N. × odorus*, the campernelle jonquil, has clusters of richly scented flowers in mid-spring. The latest to flower is *N. poeticus*, in late spring or early summer, and is excellent for naturalizing in grass.

**PROPAGATION** Division is the best method. Seed gives unpredictable results and the length of time before flowering size is reached can be over five years.

**GROWING** Rich soil and a shelterd position, possibly with a little light shade is ideal. Plant bulbs as soon as they become available, in late summer if possible. The planting hole should be three times the depth of the bulb.

**VARIETIES** 'Sweetness' *(above)*, yellow, and 'Golden Sceptre', deep yellow, are Jonquilla types. The best known Poeticus is 'Pheasant's Eye', which has white petals and a reddish cup.

**POSSIBLE PROBLEMS** Stem and bulb eelworm.

### ▮ PLANTING TIP

*To avoid root disturbance when planting out, either use pot-grown specimens or lift seed-raised plants when the rhizomes have reached finger thickness.*

### ▮ SPECIAL CARE TIP

*Allow foliage of daffodils to die down naturally. The practice of tying leaves in a knot, or cutting back should be avoided. The quality of flowers in subsequent years makes it worthwhile leaving foliage until it has turned yellow. Removing flowerheads before seed is formed also preserves vigour.*

# ACIDANTHERA

| late summer | half-hardy | full sun | 90cm/3ft | 25cm/10in |

For really exotic-looking, fragrant flowers, easily grown from corms, look no further than *A. bicolor murielae (above)*, sometimes listed as *Gladiolus callianthus*. The wide open, six-petalled white flowers have a star-like look, marked with a deep maroon at the base, and appear up to 10 at a time on slender flower spikes. They make excellent cut flowers.

**PROPAGATION** Tiny cormlets are produced around the base of the new corm, and can be removed for growing on, preferably in a nursery bed. They will take up to three years to reach their flowering size.

**GROWING** Provide full sun and a warm, sheltered spot. Well-drained soil is appreciated, but water in dry spells. Protect from frost, by lifting if necessary. Acidantheras can be grown in borders, but look particularly fine in containers.

**VARIETIES** There are no named varieties.

**POSSIBLE PROBLEMS** Storage rot *(see below)*.

# IXIA

| early summer | half-hardy | full sun | 45cm/18in | 10cm/4in |

In mild areas, the corms that produce these sprays of lovely star-shaped flowers on slender wiry stems will survive outdoors all year. In cooler climates, they can be grown under glass or planted out in spring, then lifted before the first frost for storage over winter. Ixia hybrids come in a variety of colours, but single colours are also available. They make excellent cut flowers.

**PROPAGATION** The best method is to remove cormlets that can be grown on to flowering size in the same way as the adult corms. Seed gives mixed results, but plants will reach flowering size some two years after sowing.

**GROWING** Plant in an open, sunny position in well-drained soil. Dead-head regularly.

**VARIETIES** *I. viridiflora* has green flowers, but is less vigorous than the hybrids. *I. 'venus' (above)* is an excellent variety.

**POSSIBLE PROBLEMS** Generally trouble-free.

## ▋ SPECIAL CARE TIP

*In temperate climates,* acidantheras *and various other half-hardy corms and tubers are best lifted and stored in frost-free conditions over winter. If the conditions are not right, the storage body may rot. Care should be taken not to damage them when lifting, and they should be dried well before storing.*

## ▋ PLANTING TIP

*Out of the mixture of hybrid flower colours – yellow, red, purple, blue, white and all shades in between – the yellow and white are most fragrant.*

# CROCUS

| winter | hardy | full sun | 5-8cm/2-3in | 8-10cm/3-4in |

A number of different crocus species produce scented flowers in shades of yellow, white, purple and blue. All can be relied on to provide welcome colour in winter and early spring. Undemanding plants, they will increase by themselves if happy with their conditions, but even in shady sites they will struggle to oblige. Planted under deciduous shrubs, at the front of sunny borders or in containers, they are always a delight.

**PROPAGATION** Cormlets produced by the corms can be carefully lifted and planted out separately to reach flowering size. A less exacting method is simply to lift and divide congested clumps without sorting out mature from immature corms.

**GROWING** Although very tolerant of different soils, crocus will not do well unless their site is well drained. With full sun and protection from wind and cold, they will open early and their colours can be best appreciated. Plant in autumn 8cm/3in deep and 10cm/4in apart.

**VARIETIES** For fragrance, choose *C. longiflorus*, *C. imperati* (above), *C. ancryensis* 'Golden Bunch', *C. chrysanthus* 'Snow Bunting', or *C. laevigatus*.

**POSSIBLE PROBLEMS** Mice may eat corms; birds pull them out of the ground.

# TULIPA

| spring | hardy | full sun | 30-60cm/1-2ft | 15-18cm/6-8in |

The choice of colour, flower form and size now available means that there is a tulip to suit all gardens. Some are more scented than others, but all make excellent formal spring bedding or a valuable contribution to a mixed border or cottage-style garden. They perform better as bedding if they are lifted after flowering, once the foliage turns yellow, for storage until the following early winter.

**PROPAGATION** Raising plants from seed is slow and erratic. Offsets should be removed from the bulbs when they are lifted and stored for replanting in nursery beds at the same time as the mature bulbs go in. The smaller the offset, the longer it will take to reach flowering side.

**GROWING** Alkaline soil suits tulips. Other than that, they will succeed in any soil that does not become waterlogged. Dead-head the flowers as the petals start to fall but let the leaves die down naturally.

**VARIETIES** For scent, choose 'Prince of Austria', an orange and scarlet single early, 'Orange Parrot' has the fringed petals typical of parrot types, 'Eros' (above) is a pink double late.

**POSSIBLE PROBLEMS** Bulbs in store may be eaten by mice; aphids; slugs.

## PLANTING TIP

*Although packets of mixed-colour crocus corms can be bought cheaply, the effect is better if single colours are grown in clumps. Growth is also more even.*

## ORGANIC TIP

*Remove petals that fall during dead-heading and keep the ground clear around the stems to prevent the spread of pests and diseases.*

## FREESIA

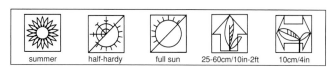

| summer | half-hardy | full sun | 25-60cm/10in-2ft | 10cm/4in |
|---|---|---|---|---|

The development of specially prepared bulbs has made it far easier to coax freesias into producing their exquisitely fragrant, funnel-shaped flowers outdoors in the first year after planting. Gardeners in mild areas have an easier time of it and can achieve excellent results with ordinary bulbs available in a wide range of named varieties and colours.

**PROPAGATION** Remove offsets from mature corms and grow on to flower, probably in the following year. Sow seeds indoors from autumn until early summer, and outdoors in summer. Soak the seeds overnight to improve germination.

**GROWING** Prepared corms should be planted in spring for flowers in late summer. Lift as the foliage starts to fade and, in subsequent years, treat as unprepared corms. In mild areas, plant corms in late summer for flowering in spring and allow to overwinter in the ground.

**VARIETIES** *F. × kewensis* 'Everett' *(above)*, crimson; 'Souvenir', yellow; 'Ballerina', white; 'Mme Curie', red. Prepared corms are usually mixtures of white, yellow, red, blue and lilac.

**POSSIBLE PROBLEMS** Aphids.

### PLANTING TIP

Freesias *can be raised under glass to flower in spring by planting unprepared bulbs in autumn. A minimum temperature of 5°C/41°F must be maintained.*

## AMARYLLIS

| late summer | half-hardy | full sun | 45-60cm/18in-2ft | 30cm/12in |
|---|---|---|---|---|

Not to be confused with the misnamed hippeastrum, commonly sold for winter and spring indoor culture, this slightly tender bulb, *A. belladonna (above)*, produces beautifully scented, pale pink, lily-like flowers in late summer and early autumn, provided it has the right conditions. An unusual feature of this plant is that the strap-shaped leaves are produced in winter or early spring but disappear shortly before the flowers take over. They last well as cut flowers.

**PROPAGATION** Seed can be sown in spring, but resulting plants take over five years to reach flowering size, and may not come true. Otherwise, lift established clumps in summer as the leaves die down, divide and replant.

**GROWING** A really sheltered position with full sun, perhaps at the base of a wall, is essential for this bulb. The soil should be fertile and kept well watered. When planting, make sure that there is 15-20cm/6-8in of soil on top of the bulb. The crown may need protection in winter.

**VARIETIES** 'Hathor' has pure white flowers.

**POSSIBLE PROBLEMS** Generally trouble-free.

### SPECIAL CARE TIP

*In cool areas, growing amaryllis is a gamble. Improve the odds by protecting the crowns in winter with coarse sand or spent potting compost.*

# CYCLAMEN

| summer | semi-shade | hardy | 8-10cm/3-4in | 10-15cm/4-6in |
|---|---|---|---|---|

There are cyclamen that flower in every season, but for strongly fragrant flowers choose *C. purpurascens*, sometimes listed as *C. europaeum*. The ground-hugging, heart-shaped leaves are beautifully veined with silvery markings and are hardy enough to last all winter through. Masses of deep pink flowers with their characteristic reflexed petals are produced from each plant. This is a beautiful plant to grow beneath deciduous trees or shrubs.

**PROPAGATION** Cyclamen corms do not produce cormlets. Seed is the only method of increase. If happy in their situation, they will self sow, but you can help by sowing fresh, ripe seed in early autumn. Germination is often slow, but prick out seedlings and grow on in a cold frame for planting out the following summer.

**GROWING** Provide some shade and plenty of moist, well-drained soil for this cyclamen. Leave undisturbed as far as possible.

**VARIETIES** *C. repandum (above)* produces scented pink flowers in spring and early summer.

**POSSIBLE PROBLEMS** Generally trouble-free in the right conditions.

# HYACINTHUS

| spring | full sun | hardy | 23cm/9in | 15cm/6in |
|---|---|---|---|---|

The scent of hyacinths is probably one of the loveliest and most unmistakable in the garden. Whether grown in borders, raised beds or containers, or indoors in pots, their fragrance, ease of cultivation and sheer beauty makes them an essential part of the spring-time garden. Any hybrid of *H. orientalis*, and there are many, will perform well and, with the right care, over several years.

**PROPAGATION** Named varieties can be propagated with offsets from the bulb, planted in a nursery bed and grown on to flowering size.

**GROWING** Specially treated bulbs can be bought for flowering early indoors, but this process exhausts the plant's reserves and it may not flower again for several years, but can be planted outside in a sheltered spot to recover. For outside displays, choose a deep, fertile soil and plant in early autumn at a depth of 12.5cm/5in.

**VARIETIES** Choose on the basis of colour: 'L'Innocence', white; 'Ostara', blue; 'City of Haarlem', yellow; 'Jan Bos', deep pink; 'Pink Pearl' *(above)*, pale pink.

**POSSIBLE PROBLEMS** Grey rot.

## ORGANIC TIP

*It is possible that bought corms may have been dug up from the wild, where their continued existence is threatened. Make sure they have been raised in this country, or even better grown from seed, which is often more reliable anyway, as bought corms are usually rather dried up, and may never come up once planted.*

## SPECIAL CARE TIP

*Pot-grown displays of forced bulbs are often spoiled by an uneven rate of growth of the bulbs, even though the same variety are used. By planting a larger number of bulbs in trays, you can select even-sized ones for potting up just before the flower buds open.*

# IRIS (RHIZOMES)

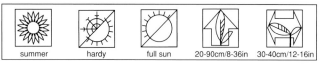

| summer | hardy | full sun | 20-90cm/8-36in | 30-40cm/12-16in |

For iris that make a dazzling statement in a herbaceous or mixed border, grow the rhizomatous types. The categories seem immensely complicated. Typically, the leaves are sword shaped, while the flowers are very characteristic in shape. Choose from bearded types, *I. germanica*, *I. pallida*, or beardless *I. graminea (above)* for summer flowers in shades of blue, purple and white. All are suitable for cutting.

**PROPAGATION** Divide rhizomes in autumn. Beardless types may not flower in the first year after division. In bearded iris, the central part of the rhizome is best discarded, as the outer parts are more vigorous.

**GROWING** Plant in well-drained, neutral soil in a sunny, open position. Plant bearded types so the tops of the rhizomes show above the soil. *I. graminea* should be planted about 5cm/2in deep and resents disturbance.

**VARIETIES** The low growing *I. unguicularis* provides an unseasonal display of large, violet-scented flowers in winter.

**POSSIBLE PROBLEMS** Generally trouble-free in the right conditions.

# IRIS (BULBS)

| late winter | hardy | full sun | 10-15cm/4-6in | 10cm/4in |

The tiny, winter-flowering irises make a heart-warming sight with their intensely coloured flowers held bravely up above sparse, greyish spikes of foliage. *I. histrioides* is the first to appear, and has very deep blue flowers with gold markings. *I. reticulata (above)* appears soon afterwards, a reliable little bulb in the harshest conditions. *I. danfordiae* has lemon-yellow flowers. All three are so low growing that they will certainly be better appreciated as pot plants, brought inside just as the flowers open, but they are also suitable for outdoor containers, front-of-border planting or rock gardens.

**PROPAGATION** In the right conditions, they will increase slowly. Otherwise, lift and divide the offsets once the foliage has died down.

**GROWING** Really good drainage is essential if these little bulbs are to survive, and an open, sunny position is appreciated. Acid soil should have a sprinkling of lime added. If the soil is not well drained, lift and store the bulbs until the following autumn, when they should be planted 5cm/2in deep.

**VARIETIES** *I. histrioides* 'Major' has good colouring; *I. reticulata* 'Cantab' has pale blue flowers. For taller summer flowers, plant *I. xiphium* which will grow to 30-60cm/1-2ft tall.

**POSSIBLE PROBLEMS** Bulb rot.

▓ SPECIAL CARE TIP

*The large flowers of* I. unguicularis *should be picked while still at the bud stage. They do unfurl quickly once they are brought inside.*

▓ PLANTING TIP

*Make a feature of early flowering bulbs by planting blue irises and yellow crocus in a sunny border, or in a raised bed where they will be conspicuous.*

## Muscari

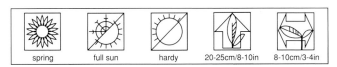

| | | | | |
|---|---|---|---|---|
| spring | full sun | hardy | 20-25cm/8-10in | 8-10cm/3-4in |

*Muscari armenaicum (above)*, or grape hyacinth, make a lovely splash of intense blue in spring in the front of borders or in rockeries, but there are other, less common types in other shades, that are even more fragrant. Most are easy to grow, and will gradually build up sizeable clumps.

**PROPAGATION** Lift and divide established clumps as the foliage starts to die down, every three or four years. Seed is another possibility, and plants will develop to flowering size in about three years.

**GROWING** Muscaris are obliging plants, but appreciate full sun, otherwise leaf is formed at the expense of flower.

**VARIETIES** *M. macrocarpum* has rich, bright yellow flowers. *M. moschatum* is very fragrant, but the flowers are a rather dull purple.

**POSSIBLE PROBLEMS** Generally trouble-free.

## Endymion

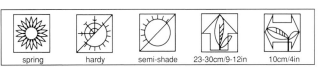

| | | | | |
|---|---|---|---|---|
| spring | hardy | semi-shade | 23-30cm/9-12in | 10cm/4in |

Few sites can equal the breathtaking loveliness of deciduous woodland carpeted with lightly fragrant bluebells. Admittedly, few gardens boast a wood in which such an effect could be reproduced, but with the increasing popularity of devoting a part of the garden to 'wild' flowers, something of the same beauty can be captured. They spread too quickly and are too untidy looking for borders. This plant is found in catalogues and reference books under a bewildering variety of names, including *E. nonscriptus*, *Scilla nonscripta*, *S. nutans* and *Hyacinthoides non-scripta (above)*.

**PROPAGATION** Plants self-seed readily. Collected or bought seed can be sown in the flowering position and left undisturbed until the plants reach flowering size in about five years. Otherwise lift and divide congested clumps, replanting immediately.

**GROWING** Moist, but not wet soil is best, although bluebells also grow in the dry shade of deciduous trees. Light shade is considered best.

**VARIETIES** Pink and white shades sometimes occur naturally. Division is the best way to continue these varieties.

**POSSIBLE PROBLEMS** Generally trouble-free.

### ▪ PLANTING TIP

The grassy foliage of muscari lasts well after the flowers have disappeared, and too long for some people's taste. This can be a problem in borders and rock gardens. They are vigorous enough to be naturalized in grass, and this allows the foliage to be disguised much more satisfactorily.

### ▪ SPECIAL CARE TIP

The bulbs of bluebells have no outer skin and this makes them vulnerable to damage and to drying out. Replant lifted bulbs straight away. The only way of buying bluebells from a nursery is to buy pot-grown plants in flower. This is expensive, but ensures that the bulbs are healthy and mature.

# PERENNIALS

**Perennials are plants whose lives extend over several years. This applies to a great many plants but, to be more precise, this chapter is concerned with hardy herbaceous perennial plants — those that have soft, rather than woody, growth.**

Some of the most popular flowering plants fall into this category, and virtually every garden includes some, from sprawling but beautifully fragrant dianthus, such as the old-fashioned pink, 'Mrs Sinkins', to stately clumps of phlox at the back of the border. Most perennials are easy to grow, easy to propagate — many can be grown from seed — and make a wonderful display at the height of summer. Many are beautifully fragrant, and have an important role to play in the aromatic garden.

Perennial borders in the grand manner came into fashion in great houses at the end of the nineteenth-century, when labour was cheap and plentiful. The kind of maintenance involved in such grand schemes,

often involving parallel borders rarely less than 3m/9ft wide and up to ten times as long, backed with brick walls or closely clipped hedges, is simply not possible for modern gardeners. Through the efforts of plant breeders, improved forms of these useful and decorative plants are now available in a huge range of colours and with a free-flowering compactness that makes them suitable for smaller gardens, so perennials can be enjoyed in less ambitious schemes.

**CHOOSING, PLANTING AND PROPAGATING PERENNIALS** The choice of perennials is a huge one, and decisions will have to be based on colour, habit, height and situation. Although many perennials do well in the same sunny, open conditions that favour annuals, some will thrive in shade, or in damp conditions; some even prefer it, so sites that seem awkward at first can often be filled using these plants.

In modern gardens, the commonest ways of displaying perennials are in island beds and mixed borders. Island beds provide an ideal way of displaying perennials on their own, where they can be viewed from all sides and are not shaded by adjacent walls or hedges. The shape of the bed can be symmetrical or informal, although the latter often looks better, and the plants are arranged with the tallest in the middle, and the shorter plants towards the edges so that all are seen to their best advantage. The disadvantage with beds composed solely of perennials is that, with a few exceptions, they die down completely in winter and the flowering season is mainly summer. This leaves quite a long period with relatively little interest, although maintenance is easier to carry out, since the routine tasks can be done for the whole border at the same time, for example, cutting back faded shoots in autumn, and dividing clumps in spring.

The mixed border is more popular in modern gardens, although it owes much of its origin to older style cottage gardens, where different types of plants were all mixed together. Like a grand herbaceous border, the mixed border is usually backed by a wall or hedge and so, unlike the island bed, it is designed to be seen from the front. The idea is to ensure that there is colour all year round, with evergreen and deciduous flowering shrubs providing a stable structure, while perennials, annuals and bulbs grow in between to provide accent points during the flowering season. It can be adapted to even the smallest gardens, although the choice of plants will be limited to those with restrained growth.

When perennials are introduced, they should be planted in groups, usually of three or five, to provide substantial blocks of colour rather than the disjointed effect produced by dotting them around singly. This takes some restraint, and you will have to restrict the number of different perennials you include, but the final effect will be far more satisfying.

Before planting perennials, it is very important to ensure that the ground is well cultivated and free of perennial weeds. This may involve a lot of digging and the application of systemic weedkillers over the growing season, but failure to eradicate perennial weeds will mean tiresome work later on. Annual weeds can be hoed out or hand pulled. Since perennials are going to stay in their flowering positions for at least three years, in most cases, the addition of well-rotted organic matter and the correction of drainage problems, by double digging if necessary, is most important. Before planting, in autumn if drainage is good, or spring in cold areas or those with heavy soil, add a base dressing of bone meal to encourage healthy root development. Feed in subsequent years with a top-dressing in spring. A mulch can be applied to an established border in mid-spring when soil is moist to conserve water and discourage weed growth. Apart from that, the major maintenance is staking. This should be started before the plants need it, so that support is there as soon as the plants show any sign of flopping over. Once they have done so, it is too late. Dead-heading throughout the season will prolong flowering.

**PERENNIALS IN THE GARDEN** There is such variety of shape, colour, habit and fragrance to choose from that the possibilities seem endless. Whatever effect you are aiming for, remember that perennials

*A border showing variety of colour, shape and fragrance.* Phlox *are ideal mid-border plants and* hemerocallis *and* bergenia *sit neatly in the front.*

bulk out considerably over the first three years after planting, so take eventual size into account.

Perennials are versatile in a way that annuals can never be, and some can perform in damp, shady locations, where annuals would certainly not thrive. A lovely pool-side planting in dappled shade could combine honey-scented hostas with the spectacular Himalayan cowslip, *Primula florindae*. In sunny, dry borders the choice is vast. Pinks are the perennials of choice for a well-drained chalky soil, where they will give of their best, tumbling over the edges of borders onto paving or gravel paths and scenting the air with cloves, under roses or as part of a silvery planting with lavender. Earlier than most perennials, peonies make a majestic statement with leathery foliage and huge flowers like saucers in early summer. These are true perennials, long lived and resenting any disturbance. The leaves remain impressive all summer, but to maintain interest in the border introduce more colour to take over from them as peonies finish flowering early.

Planting perennials is like painting with flowers, with planning and good cultivation you can colour your garden from early summer to late autumn, with one or two areas of interest in winter, too. But for the best results, careful preparation is vital.

# MORINA

| summer | half-hardy | full sun | 60-90cm/2-3ft | 45cm/18in |
|---|---|---|---|---|

# CIMICIFUGA

| summer | hardy | semi-shade | 1.2-1.5m/4-5ft | 24in/2ft |
|---|---|---|---|---|

The rather thistle-like, shiny, aromatic leaves of *M. longiflora (above)*, form a striking basal clump from which spikes of smallish flowers emerge. These appear mainly in summer, but there may be later flushes into autumn. Interestingly, the flowers start out white but age to pink and crimson and are followed by decorative green seed heads, useful for dried flower arrangements.

**PROPAGATION** Morina has a long tap-root that can be damaged if the plant is lifted for division, although this could be tried with well-established clumps. Seed is a more popular method of propagation. Sow in pots during autumn or spring, protect in a cold frame, then prick out and grow on in a nursery bed in a sheltered site before planting out the young plants the following year.

**GROWING** Choose a sunny, sheltered site with well-drained soil. Crowns will need protection from frost in cold areas.

**VARIETIES** There are no other varieties in cultivation.

**POSSIBLE PROBLEMS** Generally trouble-free.

Cimicifuga is an unusual plant with tall, graceful, plume-like spikes of white flowers that appear in mid- to late summer. Although it is not a plant for a small garden, it is perfect for the back of a lightly-shaded mixed border or for planting among trees. The flower spikes are suitable for cutting and the ferny foliage is attractive.

**PROPAGATION** Divide established clumps between mid-autumn and early spring.

**GROWING** A moist, humus-rich soil and light shade give the best results. Provide stakes to support the flower spikes in exposed situations.

**VARIETIES** *C. racemosa (above)* is the type to plant for fragrance – the other types smell unpleasant.

**POSSIBLE PROBLEMS** Generally trouble-free.

## ■ SPECIAL CARE TIP

Plants like morina, *which, besides being slightly tender, are rather unusual and sometimes difficult to find in nurseries, should be propagated each year. Use* collected seed if necessary, sown when ripe or buy from seed catalogues. This ensures a continuing supply of plants, whatever the weather conditions.

## ■ PLANTING TIP

C. foetida *smells unpleasant to humans but also, more usefully, to insects, earning it the common name bugbane. It may be worth planting this type near a* shrub or tree that is vulnerable to insect attack, but far enough away from the borders to make sure its smell is not a nuisance.

## CLEMATIS

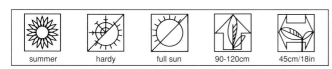

| summer | hardy | full sun | 90-120cm | 45cm/18in |

Not a climber in the wrong section, but one of the less common herbaceous clematis – C. recta (above). The white, fragrant flowers and later fluffy seed heads have the familiar clematis look, and are borne in great profusion, yet the lax, climbing stems die back to ground level in winter. It is suitable for cutting.

**PROPAGATION** Take basal cuttings in mid-to late spring and insert in pots of well-drained compost in a shady position. The plants can be planted out in autumn of the same year.

**GROWING** An alkaline soil is best, in a sunny border. Provide a mulch of well-rotted organic matter in spring.

**VARIETIES** 'Purpurea' is a purple-leaved form.

**POSSIBLE PROBLEMS** Slugs on newly emerging shoots.

## ROMNEYA

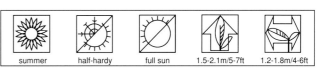

| summer | half-hardy | full sun | 1.5-2.1m/5-7ft | 1.2-1.8m/4-6ft |

This large, imposing plant with the common name of tree poppy, makes an unforgettable impression in a large garden. Each scented, white flower of R. coulteri will reach fully 12cm/5in across and has crinkled, papery petals with a prominent boss of golden yellow stamens. The greyish-green leaves are also attractive, large and deeply lobed. It can be a difficult plant. Even when the conditions seem ideal, it may sulk and fail to establish. In other gardens, it is almost too successful.

**PROPAGATION** Sow seed in early spring under glass, at about 13-16°C/55-61°F. Prick out and grow on, still in warmth. Harden off gradually and plant out in late spring of the following year. Otherwise, take root cuttings from lifted plants, although this is likely to damage the parent plant.

**GROWING** Provide a sunny position in plenty of shelter, in light, deeply cultivated soil. Help plants to get established by providing extra protection for the crown over winter.

**VARIETIES** R. trichocalyx (above) is smaller; R. 'White Cloud' is a good performer.

**POSSIBLE PROBLEMS** Generally trouble-free.

### PLANTING TIP

C. recta *needs support, ideally from a shrub, and can extend the interest of a spring-flowerer into summer or make an evergreen more decorative. Its habit means that it will not swamp the shrub, and pruning is just a matter of cutting back to just above ground level in late autumn or spring.*

### SPECIAL CARE TIP

*If the tree poppy likes its situation, it can spread beyond its allotted space. Planting it against a wall helps confine its roots and protect adjacent plants.*

## PAEONIA

|  |  |  |  |  |
|---|---|---|---|---|
| summer | hardy | full sun | 90cm/3ft | 90cm/3ft |

Peonies are a must for any herbaceous border in the traditional style. The most popular type is *P. lactiflora* , which has been widely hybridized. Massive bowl-shaped blooms rise above handsome mounds of deeply lobed leaves in early to mid-summer and give an established look to even quite young gardens, although newly planted specimens usually take more than one season to start flowering. The choice of colour and flower form are extensive.

**PROPAGATION** Peonies can be grown from seed, sown in early autumn when ripe, but named varieties will not come true, and plants will take several years to reach flowering size. Division in autumn is more common, by lifting and cutting crowns, but peonies dislike disturbance and may sulk for some time afterwards.

**GROWING** Choose moisture-retentive but well-drained soil, and cultivate deeply, incorporating well-rotted organic matter. Stake taller varieties.

**VARIETIES** 'Albert Crousse', fully double, pink flowers; 'President Roosevelt', double, deep red flowers; 'The Bride', single, white flowers with yellow stamens; 'White Wings' *(above)*.

**POSSIBLE PROBLEMS** Failure to flower.

## ACHILLEA

|  |  |  |  |  |
|---|---|---|---|---|
| summer | hardy | full sun | 45cm-1.2m/18in-4ft | 30-60cm/1-2ft |

A mainstay of the herbaceous border from early summer to early autumn, there are achilleas in many shades of yellow, as well as pink and white. Choose from upright varieties, such as *A. filipendulina*, with its 1.2m/4ft stems, most suitable for the middle or back of a border, or the more sprawling *A. taygetea* 'Moonshine', with greyish-green foliage that lasts all winter and pale, sulphur-yellow flowerheads, just right, at 45cm/18in tall, to soften the edge of a border next to a path. What they have in common are the plate-like heads of tiny, densely-packed flowers and ferny, aromatic foliage – a feature that might be missed in the taller, out-of-reach varieties.

**PROPAGATION** Divide established clumps every two or three years in mid-spring and replant immediately. Alternatively, sow seed under glass in mid-spring, prick out and grow on before planting between the following autumn and spring.

**GROWING** Achilleas must have well-drained soil and a sunny position.

**VARIETIES** *A. filipendulina* 'Gold Plate' *(above)* and 'Coronation Gold' are reliable.

**POSSIBLE PROBLEMS** Generally trouble-free.

---

### ▦ SPECIAL CARE TIP

*Peonies are a long-term investment. They live for 50 years or more without disturbance, so it is frustrating if they fail to flower. Possible causes include frost damage, root dryness or disturbance or lack of food. Choose and prepare the planting position with care, then leave them alone.*

### ▦ SPECIAL CARE TIP

*Achilleas are useful as cut flowers during summer, but even more so dried for winter arrangements. The heads of A. filipendulina are particularly suitable.*

## PRIMULA

| summer | hardy | semi-shade | 75cm-1.2m/2½-4ft | 30-38cm/12-15in |

Of all the beautiful members of the primula family, *P. florindae (above)* is certainly the most impressive. Known as the giant Himalayan cowslip, in ideal conditions it can easily top the height given here and the massive rounded heads can contain as many as 100 yellow, cowslip-scented flowers and last a good two months. It makes a distinctive amd easily grown pool-side plant.

**PROPAGATION** Established plants can be divided soon after flowering stops. Sow seed when ripe or in spring and keep well-watered. In ideal conditions, it may self-seed.

**GROWING** For the best results, plant in really moist, acid soil in partial shade. Mulch in early spring. There is no need to stake the stout stems.

**VARIETIES** Other scented primulas include *P. auricula*, often grown in shady alpine beds; *P. veris*, the cowslip, which can be naturalized in grass; and *P. vialii*, which has an upright, poker-shaped flowerhead of violet and scarlet.

**POSSIBLE PROBLEMS** Grey mould.

## OENOTHERA

| summer | hardy | full sun | 30-90cm/1-3ft | 30cm/1ft |

*Oenothera tetragona (above)* is a perennial evening primrose with the characteristic large, saucer-shaped flowers with silky yellow petals. A basal rosette of glossy green leaves gives rise to flower spikes from early summer to early autumn. The blooms are fragrant and make excellent cut flowers.

**PROPAGATION** Sow seeds in pots during spring, preferably in a sheltered position. Prick out and grow on, then plant out in autumn. Named varieties should be divided in spring.

**GROWING** Plant from autumn to spring in ordinary, well-drained soil in full sun. Keep well watered. Cut back old stems to ground level in mid autumn.

**VARIETIES** 'Fireworks' has reddish buds; 'Highlight' is very free flowering. *O. caespitosa*, white flowers freely produced over a long period, suitable for either rock gardens or front of border.

**POSSIBLE PROBLEMS** Root rot on heavy soil.

### SPECIAL CARE TIP

*Some types of primula, P. florindae for one, naturally have a coating of farina – a white, waxy powder – on flower stems, leaves and sometimes on the bases of flowers. Do not mistake this for symptoms of disease, such as grey mould. It is quite normal for some primulas and is best not disturbed.*

### PLANTING TIP

*Heavy soils really do not suit evening primroses. If, nonetheless, you are determined to grow them, improve drainage by digging in sharp grit.*

# ASPHODELINE

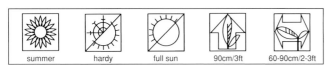

| summer | hardy | full sun | 90cm/3ft | 60-90cm/2-3ft |
|---|---|---|---|---|

The fragrant, yellow flowers of *A. lutea (above)* are star-shaped and borne in dense terminal spikes, on stiff, upright stems. These are clothed lower down with upward-pointing, narrow, grey-green leaves, with more and longer leaves emerging thickly from the base of the plant. The flowers are useful for cutting and the seed heads can be dried.

**PROPAGATION** The roots are fleshy and thick, and can easily be damaged when the clumps are lifted for division in early spring, so take care. Seed can be sown in trays of well-drained compost in spring or autumn, and pricked out into individual pots for growing on in shelter.

**GROWING** Plant in well-drained, fairly poor soil. If full sun is not available, at least ensure there is plenty of shelter.

**VARIETIES** *A. liburnica* is a smaller plant with cup-shaped flowers.

**POSSIBLE PROBLEMS** Generally trouble-free.

# HOUTTUYNIA

| summer | hardy | semi-shade | 15-23cm/6-9in | 30-45cm/12-18in |
|---|---|---|---|---|

This low-growing plant (pronounced 'who-tin-ear') makes excellent ground cover for a damp soil or poolside site and although the white flowerheads are fairly small, they show up well against the dark, citrus-smelling foliage. The fleshy roots spread rapidly underground and it can become invasive.

**PROPAGATION** Dig up sections of the root system in spring and replant in pots until healthy leaves are formed, then plant out.

**GROWING** Light shade and moist soils give the best results. If a large root spread is not wanted, plant in a dryer soil.

**VARIETIES** *H. cordata* 'Chamaeleon' *(above)* has leaves variegated with yellow and pinky-red.

**POSSIBLE PROBLEMS** Generally trouble-free.

## ▓ PLANTING TIP

*Planting* asphodel *behind blue-flowered herbaceous geraniums, such as 'Johnson's blue', provides a contrast in leaf shape, flower colour and habit.*

## ▓ SPECIAL CARE TIP

*The leaves of* houttuynia *disappear during winter, and the spread of the roots may go unnoticed. Watch for the emerging shoots and limit if necessary.*

# OSTEOSPERMUM

| summer | half-hardy | full sun | 45-60cm/18in-2ft | 30-45cm/12-18in |

These daisy-flowered perennials have recently become more popular with the development of new varieties. They make an excellent and showy feature for front-of-border sites, where the aromatic leaves will sprawl to provide ground cover. In the right conditions, the pink flowers appear all summer, but the requirements of this plant are quite exacting and losses are common in winter. Fortunately, it is very easy to propagate.

**PROPAGATION** Take cuttings at any time during the growing season. They root rapidly and easily – in fact, the stems in contact with the ground often form roots without any encouragement. Plants can also be raised from seed and germinate rapidly, but may not flower in the first year.

**GROWING** Well-drained soil and a sunny site improve the chances of osteospermum surviving through winter, although cloche protection may also be needed. Dead-head to encourage repeat flowering.

**VARIETIES** O. *jucundum (above)*; O. 'Whirligig' is a very popular, white-flowered type with rather spoon-shaped leaves.

**POSSIBLE PROBLEMS** Generally trouble-free.

# PELARGONIUM

| summer | tender | full sun | 60-90cm/2-3ft | 60cm/2ft |

The scented-leaved pelargoniums, commonly and wrongly called geraniums, have less showy flowers than the zonal, ivy-leaved or regal types, but are an excellent addition to the scented garden in summer. There are many to choose from, with leaf scents reminiscent of lemon, pepper, rose, peppermint, pine and balm. As they depend on the leaves being brushed or lightly crushed to release their perfume, and they are tender plants, it is best to grow them in raised beds or pots, where they are accessible and easily moved under cover in winter, if necessary. They will continue growing indoors as pot plants through winter and make bushy plants when mature.

**PROPAGATION** Take cuttings of non-flowering shoots (or remove flowers) any time from spring to mid-summer, cutting just below a leaf node. These should root quickly in a well-drained potting medium and can then be potted on.

**GROWING** Provide winter temperatures of at least 7°C/45°F to keep the plants growing slowly, and keep just moist. Move the plants outside after all danger of frost is past. Water and feed during the growing period.

**VARIETIES** P. *graveolens* has a rose scent; P. × *fragrans* smells of pine; P. *quercifolium (above)* has a spicy perfume.

**POSSIBLE PROBLEMS** Whitefly.

## ■ PLANTING TIP

*Planting osteospermum in a shady site will bring disappointment. Without full sun for at least part of the day, the flowers close up tightly.*

## ■ ORGANIC TIP

*Look out for whitefly when buying pelargoniums. They are easier to acquire than get rid off. Tap the leaves and watch for tiny white insects (adults) that fly up from the underside. For whitefly in a glasshouse, you can introduce the natural predator, Encarsia formosa, but this cannot be used outside in the garden.*

## DICTAMNUS

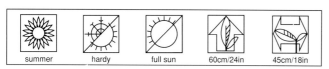

| | | | | |
|---|---|---|---|---|
| summer | hardy | full sun | 60cm/24in | 45cm/18in |

*Dictamnus albus* is sometimes known as the burning bush, for rather spectacular reasons, explained below. The dark green leaves are glossy and strong spikes of open, star-shaped white flowers appear during early and mid-summer, and the old flowerheads remain decorative. In the right conditions it is a long-lived plant and looks well in a herbaceous border.

**PROPAGATION** Dictamnus is best grown from seed sown outside when ripe in late summer or early autumn, as plants resent disturbance. It may take some months to germinate and should not be transplanted to its flowering position until about two years later.

**GROWING** Choose a well-drained, sunny site with alkaline soil. Moving established plants is risky, but plant new ones while dormant, between mid-autumn and early spring.

**VARIETIES** *D. a.* 'Purpurea' *(above)* has pink flowers with darker veining.

**POSSIBLE PROBLEMS** Generally trouble-free.

## PEROVSKIA

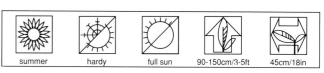

| | | | | |
|---|---|---|---|---|
| summer | hardy | full sun | 90-150cm/3-5ft | 45cm/18in |

Although a perennial, perovskia is a woody, almost shrubby looking plant. With its grey-green, toothed leaves and airy blue flower spikes up to 30cm/12in long, it makes a graceful addition to the mixed or herbaceous border. *P. atriplicifolia (above)* produces its flowers over a long period towards the end of summer, and well into autumn in the right conditions. The leaves, when crushed, have a smell reminiscent of sage.

**PROPAGATION** Increase stock by taking 10cm/3in heel cuttings in mid-summer. Root in sharply drained compost, overwinter in a frost-free location for planting out early the following spring.

**GROWING** Perovskia is an excellent choice for a seaside location and does well on chalky soil. Plant in full sun, and ensure the site is free draining. During a cold winter, leave old shoots on the plant and cut them down in spring.

**VARIETIES** 'Blue Mist' has paler blue flowers in even longer spikes, and flowers rather earlier.

**POSSIBLE PROBLEMS** Capsid bug.

### ▨ SPECIAL CARE TIP

*The reason for the common name, burning bush, can be illustrated after flowering is over. The old flower heads of dictamnus contain a fragrant oil which, on warm summer evenings forms a layer of vapour around the plant. It is possible to set light to this without, in theory, causing any harm to the plant.*

### ▨ PLANTING TIP

*The airy, greyish effect created by perovskia is a good foil for more solid-looking plants, such as tall, yellow antirrhinums (snapdragons).*

## NEPETA

| summer | hardy | full sun | 30-45cm/12-18in | 30cm/12in |

The grey-green aromatic leaves and tiny lavender-blue flowers of N. × faassenii, syn. N. mussini, form soft mounds of cloudy colour in early summer. The plant has a lax, old-fashioned look, ideal for edging paths or sprawling under shrub roses. The aroma is released when the leaves or stalks are brushed or crushed. The curious passion it seems to arouse in some cats gives it the popular name of catmint.

**PROPAGATION** Lift and divide plants in early spring, or take basal cuttings of N. mussini at the same time for planting out the following year.

**GROWING** Plant in well-drained soil in full sun. In cold areas, leave old growths on the plant until spring, then cut back to reveal the new leaves.

**VARIETIES** 'Six Hills Giant' (above) grows to about 60cm/24in; N. cataria, rather straggly, with white flowers, best grown from seed.

**POSSIBLE PROBLEMS** Generally trouble-free.

## VIOLA

| spring | hardy | full sun | 10-15cm/4-6in | 30cm/12in |

This low-growing and discreet relative of the showy garden pansy has an exquisite scent if you are prepared to get down to its level. V. odorata (above) makes perfect underplanting for rose beds, producing flowers before the roses come into bloom and spreading to provide evergreen ground cover of heart-shaped leaves. They will also spread over paving, gradually spreading their roots in the cool crevices between the stones. Long-stemmed varieties make lovely cut flowers.

**PROPAGATION** V. odorata self-seeds easily – sometimes too easily – but seedlings are easily transferred. Established clumps can also be divided in spring.

**GROWING** This viola is vigorous and easy to please, but it will perform best in fertile, moist soil in full sun or light shade. It appreciates a cool root run.

**VARIETIES** V. odorata sulphurea has yellow flowers; V. o. 'Princess of Wales' has long stems which make its violet flowers suitable for cutting; 'Coeur d'Alsace' is pink.

**POSSIBLE PROBLEMS** Generally trouble-free.

### PLANTING TIP

*If the foliage of catmint is to be used in flower arranging, it smells better before flowering. Afterwards, the scent has a mustier tone.*

### PLANTING TIP

*The sweet violet's tolerance of shade, provided drainage is good, makes it a good choice for carpeting a deciduous woodland area. Combined with common primroses and simple bulbs, like snowdrops and wood anemones, they create a natural, wild effect in a relatively short time.*

# BERGENIA

| spring | hardy | full sun | 30cm/12in | 30cm/12in |

Bergenias are one of the earliest plants to flower in a herbaceous or mixed border, and provide a year-round display, with the fragrant flowerheads in spring and large, leathery evergreen leaves that may turn red in autumn. They make excellent ground cover and are tolerant of a wide variety of soils. Both flowers and leaves are good for cutting and last very well.

**PROPAGATION** Lift and divide established clumps in autumn or mid-spring.

**GROWING** Alkaline soil is well tolerated, as is clay and even dry light shade, as well as full sun, but a poor soil in full sun gives the best leaf colour. Plant between mid-autumn and early spring but leave undisturbed as far as possible.

**VARIETIES** *B. cordifolia* has sprays of mauve-pink flowers; *B. crassifolia* has pale pink flowers that appear in early spring or even winter. Named varieties include 'Silberlight', white flowers with pink stamens; 'Ballawley' *(above)* has mauve-pink flowers.

**POSSIBLE PROBLEMS** Generally trouble-free.

# PHLOX

| summer | hardy | semi-shade | 60-120cm/2-4ft | 45-60cm/18-24in |

In late summer, *P. maculata* and *P. paniculata (above)* are excellent performers in a herbaceous or mixed border, with dense heads of flat, open flowers in shades of white, through pinks and reds to dark purple. They make excellent cut flowers and bloom freely in a variety of sites.

**PROPAGATION** Divide established clumps in autumn or spring. Basal stem cuttings can be taken in spring, or root cuttings in late winter to early spring. Plants raised from cuttings can be planted out in summer of the following year.

**GROWING** Phlox thrive in semi-shade but tolerate sun, however, flower colour is better if some shade is provided. Support in exposed areas. Mulch yearly in mid-spring to retain moisture, and water in dry periods.

**VARIETIES** *P. maculata* 'Miss Lingard', pure white flowers in tapering panicles. There are many varieties of *P. paniculata* available.

**POSSIBLE PROBLEMS** Eelworm.

## ORGANIC TIP

*An attractive combination is achieved when hostas are planted with bergenias, but the evergreen leaves of the latter may hide slugs that feast on hosta leaves. Avoid using slug pellets by making a slug trap. Sink a plastic yogurt pot halfway into the ground and pour in some beer. Slugs will be only too happy to fall in.*

## PROPAGATION TIP

*There is no cure for eelworm. Affected phlox, identifiable by their distorted shoots, should be propagated by root cuttings which are infestation free.*

# DIANTHUS (PINKS)

|  |  |  |  |  |
|---|---|---|---|---|
| summer | hardy | full sun | 25-36cm/10-15in | 22-30cm/9-12in |

The division between pinks and carnations is sometimes blurred, but through intensive hybridization two distinct groups of pinks have been formed: old-fashioned and the more vigorous, repeat flowering modern pinks, based on *D. plumarius* and *D. × allwodii* respectively. Generally speaking, they have a low, spreading habit, forming cushions of greyish foliage that lasts all year. The densely petalled flowerheads have an intense clove fragrance.

**PROPAGATION** Take cuttings from non-flowering side shoots in summer. Insert in pots of well-drained compost in a shaded place. Pot on or plant out when a healthy root system is formed. The species types can be increased by seed, preferably sown in early summer.

**GROWING** A sunny position and good drainage are important. Alkaline soil gives best results.

**VARIETIES** Species types are especially good for rock gardens, try *D. arenarius*, *D. × arvensis*, *D. caesius* or *D. noeanus*. Old-fashioned pinks, 'Laced Joy' *(above);* 'Mrs Sinkins', white with a wonderful fragrance; 'Inchmery', pale pink; 'Gran's Favourite', white with dark lacing. Modern pinks, 'Doris', pale pink with red ring near centre; 'Haytor', white.

**POSSIBLE PROBLEMS** Generally trouble-free.

# DIANTHUS (CARNATIONS)

|  |  |  |  |  |
|---|---|---|---|---|
| summer | hardy | full sun | 60-90cm/2-3ft | 36-45cm/15-18in |

Hardy perennial border carnations were developed from *D. caryophyllus*, the clove pink, as were the annual, bedding forms and the perpetual-flowering carnations, which are raised under glass. The outdoor perennial types have the typical grey-green leaves of the dianthus family, but the flowers differ from those of most pinks in that the petals have smooth edges. They have an upright habit, and flower generously in mid-summer, with each stem carrying up to five flowers.

**PROPAGATION** Sow seed as for pinks, although named varieties are best increased by layering, preferably from young plants, in mid- to late summer. Roots should have formed after six weeks, and the new plants can be lifted a month later.

**GROWING** The same conditions as for pinks give the best results. These are good mid-border plants, best planted in spring or autumn. Stake carefully.

**VARIETIES** 'Imperial Clove', violet-carmine; 'Merlin Clove', white with crimson marking; 'Perfect Clove', deep crimson; 'Scarlet Lunette' *(above),* deep red.

**POSSIBLE PROBLEMS** Carnation fly.

## SPECIAL CARE TIP

*Modern pinks sometimes go on producing flower buds in the depths of winter. These should be removed promptly, as they will produce poor quality flowers in spring, and possibly delay the start of flowering in summer. Do not apply an organic mulch to pinks as this may cause rotting of the stems.*

## SPECIAL CARE TIP

*For the largest flowers, retain only terminal buds on main stems and side shoots and remove the rest. Replace the plants every two or three years.*

# HOSTA

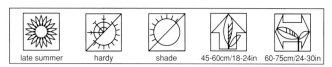

| late summer | hardy | shade | 45-60cm/18-24in | 60-75cm/24-30in |

Hostas are useful perennials, because they grow well in shade and damp soil. The foliage is attractive in itself, particularly the variegated types, and the racemes of nodding, bell-like flowers, usually in shades of white or lilac, are a bonus. This is particularly so when, as in the case of *H. plantaginea*, the white flowers, set off by glossy yellowish foliage, are scented. In the right conditions, the leaves make lush ground cover.

**PROPAGATION** Hostas can be grown from seed but, as they rarely come true to type, division of the crowns is better. Lift, divide and replant in early spring, as growth is starting.

**GROWING** Plant between mid-autumn and early spring in partial shade. Soil should be moisture retaining, but not water-logged, and fairly rich. A waterside or woodland planting is ideal. Hostas are long-lived plants and can be left undisturbed for many years.

**VARIETIES** *H. p. grandiflora (above)*; 'Honeybells' has green leaves and deep lilac, fragrant flowers.

**POSSIBLE PROBLEMS** Slugs and snails.

# HEMEROCALLIS

| summer | hardy | full sun | 60-90cm/2-3ft | 60-90cm/2-3ft |

A useful and vigorous plant, producing clumps of strap-like leaves that, in some varieties, are semi-evergreen. Branching flower stalks rise above the foliage in mid-to late summer, and although each flower lasts only a day – giving rise to the common name, day lily – new buds are constantly being formed. Some varieties are more fragrant than others. *H. flava*, syn. *H. lilio-asphodelus*, produces well-perfumed, pale yellow flowers rather earlier than most.

**PROPAGATION** Species types may come true from seed, but named varieties will not. It is better to divide established clumps in autumn or spring.

**GROWING** Provide full sun or very light shade and good, moist soil. Plant between autumn and spring. Day lilies make good pool-side plants and are attractive mid-border specimens, but avoid root disturbance unless propagating.

**VARIETIES** Other fragrant day lilies include *H. dumortieri*, with golden, brown-backed flowers, *H. minor*, similar but smaller; 'Burning Daylight' *(above)*, deep orange flowers; 'Marion Vaughn', pale-lemon, green-centred flowers.

**POSSIBLE PROBLEMS** Slugs can damage young foliage.

## ORGANIC TIP

*Hedgehogs, frogs and toads enjoy a meal of slugs and snails. Encourage them into your garden and give up using slug pellets. A barrier of sawdust, wood ash or soot around the hostas also discourages slugs and snails, but renew it regularly. Otherwise, grow hostas in pots, but water regularly.*

## ORGANIC TIP

*In a pool-side planting, slugs can be kept under control if frogs are introduced. Once day lilies are established, the problem is less marked.*

# ACORUS

| 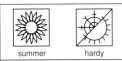 |  |  |  |  |
|---|---|---|---|---|
| summer | hardy | semi-shade | 60-70cm/2-2½ft | 45cm/18in |

The insignificant yellow green flowers that appear in summer are not the real attraction of this semi-evergreen, poolside plant; the richly aromatic, rush-like leaves make it well worth growing. They were used, along with other aromatics, for scattering on the floors of medieval castles to sweeten the air when crushed underfoot. The sweet, spicy fragrance released earns it the name sweet flag.

**PROPAGATION** Lift and divide established clumps about every three or four years in spring.

**GROWING** Plant in a sunny, open site, with the roots underwater or in poolside water that does not dry out.

**VARIETIES** *A. calamus* 'Variegatus' *(above)* has variegated foliage.

**POSSIBLE PROBLEMS** Generally trouble-free.

# VERBENA

|  |  |  |  |  |
|---|---|---|---|---|
| summer | half-hardy | full sun | 10cm-1.5m/4in-5ft | 30-60cm/1-2ft |

The large range of possible sizes for verbenas give a hint at the varied habits of these plants. There are upright forms, suitable for the back of perennial borders, sprawling types that are best with their shoots pegged down to scramble over rock gardens, and small, bushy, front-of border specimens. What they all have in common is their dense and profuse clusters of primrose-scented flowers that make them so popular for summer bedding.

**PROPAGATION** Although perennial, most verbenas can be successfully grown from seed to flower in the first year. Sow in late winter under glass, at about 18°C/65°F. Prick out, and harden off carefully before planting out.

**GROWING** Plant in a sunny, open position and water during dry spells. Dead-head to prolong flowering. To overwinter plants outside, provide protection for the roots with cloches if there is any danger of frost.

**VARIETIES** *V. bonariensis* is a tall, upright form with lavender-pink flowers; *V. rigida* is a shorter, more bushy type with purple or white flowers; *V. peruviana (above)* has sprawling stems with scarlet flowers.

**POSSIBLE PROBLEMS** Generally trouble-free.

## ▨ PLANTING TIP

As part of a planting scheme for a water feature, acorus provides the much-needed shelter for beneficial tadpoles and the frogs that will eat slugs.

## ▨ PLANTING TIP

If container-grown, verbenas can easily be moved into a sheltered area during winter and will have a better chance of surviving cold weather.

Cutting back in spring will help the plant remain bushy.

# ROSES

**Roses have a special place in the hearts of gardeners, add to that a uniquely romantic history and symbolism and you can appreciate how irrestible they can be.**

To describe roses as flowering shrubs seems to be quite inadequate. Combined with beauty of flower and form is an adaptability and resilience that makes all varieties of roses particurlarly useful, and to top it all their fragrance is unsurpassed.

The genus Rosa is a large one, with some 3,000 species although  very few of those are cultivated in gardens. Roses grow in very varied habitats, from temperate to tropical regions. This hardiness provides a ray of hope to gardeners in difficult situations. From over 1,000 cultivars there is almost sure to be a rose that will do — in fact, the only condition that no rose will thrive in is dense shade. The variety of habit is astounding, too. From huge and vigorous ramblers, such as *Rosa filipes* 'Kiftsgate', to tiny miniatures, there are roses to suit every garden.

The variety can seem overwhelming, but despite the many named groups, the choice, as far as bush roses go, is between two basic types distinguished more by their appearance and habit than their history: modern and shrub roses. Modern cultivars, previously known as hybrid-tea and floribunda roses, now reclassified as large-flowered and cluster-flowered bush roses, offer a range of colour and a capacity of repeat flowering that would have been unimaginable a hundred years ago. Shrub roses, something of a misleading term, since all roses are shrubs, can be considered to include real old roses, some of which do not repeat flower, and with a colour range restricted to pinks, reds, crimsons, purples and whites, as well as more recent cultivars with a wider range of colours, but still maintaining the soft flower shape and exquisite scent of the older types. Ramblers are similar in style to old-fashioned roses, while climbers exist in both modern and old-fashioned types. The roses in this chapter are listed by historical development from the simple species rose to the highly developed miniature.

**BUYING AND PLANTING ROSES**   A good way to set about choosing roses is to visit a rose nursery or garden in the summer, when you can see them in bloom, then place your order with a specialist grower. Container-grown plants can be planted at any time, except when the soil is water-logged, and bare-rooted roses, the form favoured by specialist nurseries, should be planted in the dormant season, avoiding frosts.

Roses do well in a neutral soil, but tolerate slight variations in soil pH. Good drainage and, ideally, full sun will allow them to thrive, and well-rotted organic matter and bonemeal can be added to the planting hole, which should be wider than the spread of the roots and some 30cm /1ft deep. In spring and midsummer a rose fertilizer, with extra potash to encourage flowers, should be applied as a top dressing.

**PROPAGATING ROSES** Few amateur gardeners ever attempt to propogate roses themselves, but good results can be achieved with persistance and experience. Indeed, rose propogation can develop into a fascinating hobby. The main mehtods used are budding, cuttings, layering and seed. Most modern roses are not grown on thier own roots, but are grafted onto vigorous rootstocks. Propogation would involve inserting a bud from the chosen variety or scion into a specially grown seedling rootstock, a rather delicate operation. Species roses may come true from seed, but cross-pollination by insects can give unexpected results. Layering is a relatively simple operation, and is suitable for roses with flexible stems, such as ramblers or many shrub roses. Hardwood cuttings of species roses and of some varieties can give good results, often improved by the use of a rooting hormone before they are inserted in the slit trench.

**PRUNING AND MAINTENANCE** The principles of pruning are simple. The harder the pruning, the fewer but larger the flowers produced. Bush roses, whether large-flowered or cluster-flowered, should be pruned fairly hard in early spring to just above an outward-facing bud using sharp,clean secateurs. The idea is to form well-branched, open-centred bushes with no crossing branches. As a rule of thumb, reducing the length of shoots by about half should result in healthy plants. The only other pruning that bush roses need is regular dead-heading to remove flower heads and encourage further flowering and, perhaps in exposed areas, heading-back in late autumn, when taller bushes can be reduced in height by about one third, to prevent wind rock.

Shrub roses need far less pruning. Diseased or damaged shoots should be cut out at any time of year, as with any shrub, and some of the oldest growth can be removed annually on established shrubs to encourage new shoots from the base. Climbers and ramblers need slightly different treatment, but for detailed instructions a specialist rose book is recommended. Basically, climbers flower on side growths that emerge from a framework of main stems. By training main stems out in a fan shape, or even horizontally, more side growths are encouraged. After flowering, these side growths should be pruned back to within two or three buds of the main stem. Most ramblers can be left alone, and as their prickles may be fierce the majority of gardeners opt for this policy, but removing some of the oldest shoots from the base of an established rambler, again after flowering, can only do it good. One principle that applies to all roses is that of removing and disposing of prunings hygienically, preferably by burning. Roses are subject to many pests and diseases, and cleanliness is one of the best ways of preventing their spread.

**ROSES IN THE GARDEN** Since even the most repeat-flowering roses only really flower during the summer and autumn, there are long periods of no interest. To have a large bed devoted solely to roses, therefore, is really only an option for those with large gardens, but a smaller bed can be successfully planned with a choice of patio or other small roses. Beds containing a single cultivar have tremendous impact, but where lack of space makes this impractical, it is very important to match the roses for height, habit and if possible, colour.

An exciting idea, but one that really does take up space, is the formal rose garden, perhaps enclosed with climbers and ramblers on screens, pergolas or walls, with winding paths leading between beds of old-fashioned roses and standards. A garden like this would be a major project in terms of maintenance and expense and not recommended for the faint-hearted.

To move from one extreme to another, roses can be grown quite successfully in containers. Obviously, smaller cultivars, especially miniatures are well suited for this, but again the lack of interest at certain times of year is a disadvantage. One way of overcoming this problem in the garden is to include roses in mixed borders. Shrub roses are the most suitable type for this, as their more natural shape combines well with other shrubs, perennials and annuals. Planting evergreens, winter-flowering pansies and bulbs extends the season of interest for the whole border.

Vertical features can be enhanced with climbing or rambling roses and can even be planted to form robust and impenetrable hedges. Shrub varieties such as Rugosa and Alba roses are excellent for this, growing into dense spiny barriers with exquisitely fragrant blooms in summer, and some have the added bonus of decorative hips later in the season.

ROSES

## SPECIES

summer   hardy   full sun   varies   varies

Species roses are those which are found growing wild, or natural crosses between two or more such species. All modern roses are descended from them. Some species have given rise to groups named after them, such as the albas, centifolias, moss roses and others which are described separately. There are many others which are easy to obtain and which make beautiful, hardy, disease-resistant shrubs with an interesting history.

**VARIETIES** *Rosa. × odorata* (Tea rose), 3m/10ft, hybrid bearing fragrant, creamy-pink flowers from mid-summer for up to four months. *R. × paulii*, thicket-forming up to 1.2m/4ft high but spreading three times as wide. A valuable ground-cover rose bearing clusters of fragrant white flowers throughout the summer. A pink form is available. *R. primula (above)* 2.4m/8ft, abundant pale yellow blooms, particularly fragrant at night; the leaves smell of myrrh when crushed. *R. wichuriana* (Memorial rose), prostrate, arching growth, white fragrant flowers from high summer for three months. *R. banksiae* (Banks's rose), very vigorous climber to 12m/40ft in sheltered conditions, double, white, sweetly scented flowers in summer, followed by round red hips; *R. b. lutea* is a yellow-flowered variety.

## GALLICA

summer   hardy   full sun   1.5m/5ft   1.2m/4ft

*Rosa gallica* is the oldest of the species, originating from Persia, and is the parent of many old garden roses. The species is prickly and bristly, with crimson-pink flowers, which give one good showing in mid-summer. This is the case with all gallica types. They make dense shrubs of dark green foliage, and many are sweetly perfumed.

**VARIETIES** *R. g. officinalis (above)*, a double-flowered form, the famous red rose of Lancaster or Apothecary's rose, best planted in groups; *R. g.* 'Versicolor' syn. 'Rosa Mundi' is a striped pink and white sport, good for hedging; *R.g. pumila*, dwarf prostrate form with red flowers; 'Rose du Maitre d'Ecole', 1.2m/4ft, large, quartered mauve blooms fading to lavender; 'Gloire de France', 90cm/3ft, good for small gardens, abundant bowl-shaped pink flowers; 'Camaieux', 1.2m/4ft, bowl-shaped white flowers striped red; 'Charles de Mills' 1.5m/5ft, the best gallica, open, quartered, maroon flower.

■ PLANTING TIP

*Although species roses, with a few exceptions, flower once in the season, many have the added attraction of decorative hips borne in the autumn.*

R. sericea pteracantha *has many attractions – ferny foliage, large and decorative ruby-red thorns, dainty white flowers, followed by red hips.*

■ PLANTING TIP

*The short flowering season of* gallica *roses makes them particularly suitable for growing in a mixed border, planned to extend the period of interest.*

82

## DAMASK

| summer | hardy | full sun | 90cm-1.5m/3-5ft | 90cm-1.5m/3-5ft |

One of the earliest written records of *Rosa damascena* is from the pen of the Latin poet Virgil, and it was certainly known to the Greeks. The foliage is grey-green and the double flowers, borne in flat-topped clusters, curve inwards; pink in bud, they fade to white. Portland damasks are hybrids from a crossing with the China rose, from which they derive their quality of continuous flowering. All damasks need to be pruned hard.

**VARIETIES** 'Versicolor' ('York and Lancaster'), 1.2 x 1.2m/4 x 4ft, floppy, semi-double flowers, white splashed pink or all pink, of interest to collectors, but not a strong grower. 'Madame Hardy', 1.5 x 1.5m/5 x 5 ft, exquisite, full-petalled, flat-faced white with a green eye. 'Comte de Chambord' (Portland), 1.2m x 90cm/4 x 3ft, reliable variety with a long flowering period, full rose-pink bloom with ruffled petals, outstanding fragrance. *R. d.* 'Bifera', 1.5 x 1.2m/5 x 4ft, called the Autumn damask because of its second flowering, fabulous, ruffled, semi-double, sugar-pink flowers, highly scented. 'Rose de Resht' (Portland) *(above)*, 90 x 90cm/3 x 3ft, low-growing compact shrub with crimson pompon blooms, strong scent; good for small gardens.

## ALBA

| summer | hardy | semi-shade | 1.8m/6ft | 1.2m/4ft |

The group of old roses which are known as albas are derived from *Rosa × alba*, a hybrid between the damask and dog rose. The latter gives albas an unmatchable toughness among roses — they can cope with (indeed thrive on) poor soil and in semi-shade, and are very long-lived. Many varieties are known for their fragrance. *R. × alba suavolens* is an important source of attar of roses. If pruned hard, albas even do well in windy situations. They flower once, in summer, and are in white or shades of pink — outstanding shrubs for the cottage garden or for a white scheme.

**VARIETIES** 'Felicité Parmentier', 1m/3ft 6in, pale pink, petals open flat then reflex into a sphere, soft grey-green foliage; 'Konigin von Danemark' *(above)*, 1.8m/6ft, makes a fine specimen with soft pink, quartered blooms — the finest alba; 'Celestial', 1.8m/6ft, pure pink, semi-double flowers emerge from exquisite buds; 'Maiden's Blush', may reach 2.4m/8ft, warm pink, rounded blooms shading to cream at the edges; 'Mme Plantier', 1.8m/6ft free-standing but 5m/15ft if climbing, bears masses of full, white blooms; 'Belle Amour', 1.5m/5ft, clusters of spicily scented, pale salmon-pink flowers.

### ■ SPECIAL CARE TIP

*Strong-growing damasks can be encouraged to produce more flowers if some of the taller canes are gently bent outwards and pegged down, so that they arch towards the ground. This will result in flowers being formed all along the canes rather that just in inaccessible clusters at the top of the shrub.*

### ■ PLANTING TIP

*Albas have fewer thorns than many other classes of rose, but are very hardy, so are suitable for gardens in which children play. They are almost disease-free, so use of sprays can be avoided altogether. For a small garden, 'Amelia', 'Felicite Parmentier' and 'Pompon Blanc Parfait', are all ideal at 1.2m/4ft tall.*

## CENTIFOLIA

summer · hardy · full sun · 90cm-1.5m/3-5ft · 90 cm-1.5m/3-5ft

## MOSS

summer · hardy · full sun · 1.8m/6ft · 1.5m/5ft

*Rosa × centifolia*, the Provence or cabbage rose, is a hybrid of ancient, probably Moorish origin, and has long been cultivated in Europe not only for its beauty but commercially for rose oil. Having been introduced to the Spanish, it was taken to the Netherlands in the seventeenth-century. Because many Dutch flower paintings include centifolias, they became known as *La Rose du Peintre*. Pinks and carmines predominate among the varieties, all of which are blessed with a unique richness of perfume. They flower once, in mid-summer, and need hard pruning to achieve a good shrubby shape. Left to themselves centifolias become awkwardly tall.

**VARIETIES** 'Fantin Latour' *(above)*, 1.5m/5ft, named after the great French painter, delicious pale pink, full flat blooms, dark green foliage. As a climber it can reach 3m/10ft. 'Tour de Malakoff' (the Taffeta rose), up to 2.1m/7ft, deep, almost magenta pink, fading to soft lilac-grey, a large, full, loosely formed bloom, vigorous upright grower with large glossy leaves. *R. × cristata* ('Chapeau de Napoleon'), pink, called the crested rose because of its winged calyces. 'Bullata', 75cm/2ft 6in, pink, full-flowered with distinctive crinkled leaves, like lettuce. 'Pompon de Bourgogne', 90cm/3ft, tiny wine-red flowers, good for containers.

Moss roses get their name from the moss-like covering of the bud. They derive from *R. centifolia muscosa*, the true moss rose. The flowers are sweeetly scented, the 'moss' redolent of balsam, which makes an intriguing contrast. Most flower once, in mid-summer, but there are some repeat-flowering varieties. The parent bears pink flowers; the varieties are shades of pink or white. They range in size from dwarfs to very tall, offering something for most gardens. Like the hybrid perpetuals, they were very popular with the Victorians.

**VARIETIES** 'Henri Martin' *(above)*, 1.8m/6ft, vivid crimson flowers, light green moss; 'Salet', 1.2m/4ft, continuous-flowering, bright pink; 'William Lobb', 1.8m/6ft or more, buds thick with moss, dramatic purple-magenta bloom; 'General Kleber', 1.5m/5ft, thick moss, double clear pink blooms with yellow stamens; 'Mousseline' syn. 'Alfred de Dalmas', 1.2m/4ft, repeat-flowering, pale pink clusters, compact shape; 'Mme de la Roche-Lambert', 1.2m/4ft, repeat-flowering, full, mauve-pink flowers, brown moss; 'Comtesse de Murinais', 1.8m/6ft, white flowers with a green eye.

■ SPECIAL CARE TIP

*Centifolias have such large, fully double flowers, often on rather lax stems, that they can be weighed down in mid-summer with the sheer profusion of flower.*

*Provide discreet support around the base of the rose fairly soon after planting to keep the stems more upright and thus make the flowers more accessible.*

■ PLANTING TIP

*The moss that develops on the buds of moss roses may be scented and extends the period of interest of these roses beyond the mainly mid-summer flowering time.*

## CHINA

| summer-autumn | hardy | full sun | 60cm-2.4m/2-8ft | 60-90cm/2-3ft |
|---|---|---|---|---|

China roses originate from varieties cultivated in China for centuries before they were first introduced into Europe, during the late eighteenth-century. They introduced an important characteristic of repeat flowering, that rose breeders were quick to make use of – many varieties of *Rosa chinensis* were developed and still make valuable garden plants for a sunny, sheltered site. They have a dainty, twiggy look, best planted with others of the same type, since the coarser types, such as rugosas, would overpower them completely.

**VARIETIES** 'Old Blush China' *(above)* is particularly important historically, as it was one of the first of the type to be imported, but earns its place in the garden with a long flowering period, from mid-summer to winter in favourable conditions, and the sweet-pea scent of the lax, pink flowers. In a border it grows to 1.2m/4ft, but against a warm wall, will reach 2.4m/8ft or more. 'Cramoisi Superieur' has deep crimson flowers and reaches just 90cm/3ft. 'Irene Watts' is a tiny rose, just 60cm/2ft tall, with fully double, pale peach flowers.

## BOURBON

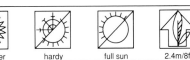

| summer | hardy | full sun | 2.4m/8ft | 1.2m/4ft |
|---|---|---|---|---|

Of all the so-called 'old roses' (those which were produced from hybridization of the species and predate the modern hybrid tea), the bourbon is the most distinctive in shape. The blooms are cup-shaped, rather like a peony, red, pink or white and measure 7.5cm/3in across. Bourbons descend from the China rose, which is responsible for the long flowering period from early summer to the first frosts, and the damask, which bestows on all bourbons a rich scent. The name comes from the Isle of Bourbon (Réunion) where the first bourbon was discovered in the nineteenth-century.

**VARIETIES** 'Boule de Neige', 1.2m/4ft, groups of three-four small, ball-shaped white flowers; 'Mme Isaac Pereire' *(above)*, 1.8m/6ft, vigorous variety which may be grown as a climber, carmine-red blooms; 'Variegata de Bologna', once-flowering but worth it, white with cerise-purple stripes, upright to 2.1m/7ft; 'Mme Pierre Oger' 1.5m/5ft, Ravishing, creamy pink, water-lily-like blooms; 'Louise Odier', deep mauve-pink, enticing scent; 'Zigeuner Knabe', to 2.4m/8ft, once-flowering with deep purplish pink flowers followed by bright vermilion hips; 'Souvenir de la Malmaison', 1.5m/5ft, creamy pink, double, quartered blooms, intense fragrance - a superb rose.

## SPECIAL CARE TIP

*Like most species and shrub roses, Chinas need very little pruning. Just dead-head to promote continued flowering, and remove dead, old or weak wood.*

## PLANTING TIP

*A number of bourbon climbers are available and, with their large, old-fashioned looking flowers in soft shades, make a far better choice for an old house than the stiffer modern climbers. The climbing version of 'Souvenir de la Malmaison' has even larger flowers than the shrub.*

# Hybrid Perpetuals

| | | | | |
|---|---|---|---|---|
| | hardy | full sun | 1.8m/6ft | 1.2m/4ft |

Modern large-flowered bush roses owe their quality of repeat-flowering to hybrid perpetuals and – in the case of the pinks and reds – their strong fragrance too. Hybrid perpetuals themselves are the result of crosses between the Portland damask, bourbon and China roses. The flowers open in clusters. The Victorians loved them and today's gardeners still value these beautiful shrubs, though the tallest kinds can be difficult to site. The back of a border or against a wall is best. The deep colours are prone to fade in full sun.

**VARIETIES** 'Paul Neyron', 1.2m/4ft, peony-shaped, pale pink blooms; 'Souvenir du Dr Jamain', 1.5m/5ft, deep damson-purple, shapely blooms, intense fragrance; 'Baroness Rothschild', 1.6m/5ft 6in, reaches 3m/10ft as a climber, large, rounded, sugar-pink flowers; 'Baron Girod de l'Ain' *(above)*, 1.5m/5ft, deep magenta blooms finely edged with white, very strong scent; 'Empereur du Maroc', 1m/3ft 6in, needs warmth and shelter to produce very dark wine-red, open flowers with a heady scent.

# Rugosa

| | | | | |
|---|---|---|---|---|
| summer | hardy | full sun | 2.1m/7ft | 1.8m/6ft |

Rugosa roses are distinguished by their foliage, which is shiny, strong and deeply veined. The true species 'Rubra' is a dense vigorous shrub reaching about 1.8m/6ft in height. It bears very large, single blooms of a brilliant crimson red, followed by bright red hips. 'Alba' is a white-flowered form. Native to Japan, the rugosas were introduced to Europe in 1779. The stems are strong and thorny, the leaves disease-resistant; for all their vigour the plants produce flowers with an enchanting air of delicacy. They are happy in partial shade and in poor soil.

**VARIETIES** 'Roseraie de la Hay' *(above)*, introduced in 1901 and named after a famous garden in France; very large purplish crimson blooms, are loosely formed with a rich fragrance; continuous-flowering, foliage bronzed in autumn. 'Blanc Double de Coubert', introduced in 1892, 1.8 x 1.5m/6 x 5ft semi-double, pure white blooms. A free-flowering shrub with beautiful dark green foliage. These two are good hedging plant – set them 1.2m/4ft apart. 'Agnes', a cross with *R. foetida* has produced this yellow hybrid, a colour rarely seen among old roses. The double flowers make one good show in the summer. Smaller than most rugosas at 1.2 x 1.2m/4 x 4ft.

■PLANTING TIP

*The mid-summer flowering of the striped* gallica, *'Rosa Mundi', seems all too brief. For a long show of similar blooms try hybrid perpetual 'Ferdinand Pichard'.*

■PLANTING TIP

*With their spiny stems and dense growth, rugosas are excellent for planting as hedges and rapidly form a fragrant, impenetrable and decorative barrier*

## SWEET BRIARS

| summer | hardy | full sun | 1.5-4m/5-12ft | 1.5-3m/5-10ft |

This class of rose, classified under *Rosa eglanteria*, is commonly known as the Sweet or Penzance Briar, and was first raised at the end of the nineteenth-century from a cross involving *R. foetida*, which gave the variety their apple-scented, bright green foliage. The shrubs are vigorous and thorny, excellent for making tall, informal hedges in a large garden. The flowers are very freely borne, saucer-shaped and sweetly scented, followed, in many varieties, by shiny red hips that last well. Sweet briars will tolerate poor conditions better than most roses and can be pruned hard in late autumn to encourage production of the aromatic foliage, or left unpruned for the best display of flowers and hips.

**VARIETIES** *R. eglanteria* grows to a dense shrub 2.4m/8ft tall and wide, with single, pink flowers and very aromatic foliage. Excellent varieties include 'Lady Penzance', coppery-pink flowers; 'Lord Penzance', buff-yellow; 'Janet's Pride', pink with a white centre; 'Amy Robsart' *(above)*. They are all about 1.8m/6ft tall and wide.

## TEAS

| summer-autumn | slightly tender | full sun | 1.2-9m/4-30ft | 1.2-6m/4-20ft |

This class of rose was developed in China from a cross between *Rosa chinensis* and *R. gigantea*. Just two were introduced into Europe, but formed the basis for the whole group and one of the parent-types for the ever popular hybrid teas. Tea roses are either climbers or shrubs, and their beautiful, spicily-scented flowers, mostly pink or pale yellow, repeat very well. The hardier types need a sheltered, sunny spot while the most tender are inaccessible to those in temperate climates, unless grown under glass.

**VARIETIES** 'Souvenir de Mme Leonie Viennot' is one of the hardier climbers, reaching 3m/10ft, with large, very scented flowers in primrose with a pale copper flush; 'Lady Hillingdon' *(above)* has apricot-yellow flowers, beautifully shaped and scented, and reaches 4.5m/15ft; 'Sombreuil' climbs to 4m/12ft, and has pure white flowers of great beauty, repeating well in autumn; 'Mme Berkley' is a bush type, free flowering with salmon pink and gold flowers, just 90cm/3ft tall.

## ▨ SPECIAL CARE TIP

*It is difficult to grow roses organically. In a healthy garden, aphids are eventually killed by ladybirds and hoverflies, but fungus diseases pose more of a problem. Mildew, black spot and rust spread rapidly if untreated. Use a fungicide without added insecticide, or you may kill beneficial insects.*

## ▨ PLANTING TIP

*Both the climbers and the bush roses of this slightly tender type are best grown with the shelter of a sunny wall, which will give them protection from cold winds.*

## SMALL CLUSTER-FLOWERED BUSH

| summer | hardy | full sun | 60cm/24in | 60cm/24in |

These roses, once known as hybrid polyanthas, bear their blooms in clusters, many of them opening at the same time. In recent years, low-growing cultivars, sometimes called 'patio roses' by commercial growers have been introduced. At up to 60cm/24in high, neat and compact in form, they are well suited to small beds or to container growing. The colour range is extensive.

**VARIETIES** 'Pretty Polly', a prizewinner in 1989, with soft pink, full rounded blooms; 'Kim', dwarf with very full canary yellow blooms and small, matt green leaves. Excellent for tubs and boxes; 'Charleston', lightly fragranced, but a good choice where eye-catching colour is wanted, with yellow and crimson flowers suffused crimson as they age; 'Pernille Poulssen', early-flowering, salmon-pink blooms turn pale as they age; 'Escapade' *(above)*, musk-scented, single, lilac-rose blooms with a white centre; 'Yvonne Rabier', first introduced in 1910 and still worth seeking out, white, full blooms, neat glossy foliage; 'Sweet Magic', small sculpted flowers of orange and yellow, only 45cm/18in high.

## LARGE CLUSTER-FLOWERED BUSH

| summer | hardy | full sun | 1.2m/4ft | 90cm/3ft |

These large cluster-flowered roses — those reaching about 75cm/2ft 6in or a little more — lend themselves to various styles of planting. Pruned to a shapely outline, they can be grown in containers. They fit well into mixed borders but, like large-flowered roses, also look good in beds devoted to roses or as an informal hedge. In these situations, the best effect is achieved by limiting yourself to one colour or even one variety. Taller, more vigorous types vary in height from 1.2m/4ft to 1.8m/6ft (though this is unusual). These too may be used as hedges or at the back of a border. All those listed are sweetly scented, bear their blooms in clusters and should be pruned hard in spring

**VARIETIES** Medium; 'Amber Queen', saffron yellow; 'Korresia', rich yellow, the best bedding rose; 'Ann Aberconway', apricot-yellow; 'Buck's Fizz', clear soft orange; 'Elizabeth of Glamis' *(above)*, coral pink; 'Ann Livia', sugar-pink; 'Scented Air', salmon-pink; 'Shocking Blue', magenta; 'Lilli Marlene', scarlet; 'Trumpeter', vermilion-scarlet; 'Margaret Merril', white. Tall: 'Arthur Bell', golden yellow; 'Chinatown', yellow tinted pink; 'Circus', yellow shaded salmon; 'Moon Maiden', creamy yellow, very full with 55 petals; 'Iceberg', white; 'Korona', orange; 'Orange Sensation'; 'Southampton', apricot, excellent for cutting; 'Vera Dalton', pale rose; 'Ma Perkins', deep pink full blooms.

### ▨ SPECIAL CARE TIP

*Roses can be grown in containers, and for such small specimens it is probably the best way of presenting them. But in the hot, dry and sunny conditions that exist on most patios, watch out for mildew and red spider mite. Make sure the roses are well watered and fed to improve disease resistance.*

### ▨ PLANTING TIP

*The habit of cluster-flowered roses makes them better for planting in mixed borders than large-flowered, which really look best in a bed of their own.*

## LARGE-FLOWERED BUSH

| summer | hardy | full sun | 1.8m/6ft | 1.2m/4ft |
|--------|-------|----------|----------|----------|

This group of roses is probably still the most popular for smaller gardens. They are the result of crossing hybrid perpetual varieties with tea-scented roses and were introduced in the late nineteenth-century. They are very hardy, strong growers, and with a long flowering season - from early summer to late autumn. Light pruning produces more flowers; gardeners after a few prize blooms will prune hard to concentrate the plant's energies to that effect. In the typical flower shape, the outer petals curve outwards from a pointed centre. The colour range is vast, but as a rule the deep reds and rich pinks (descendants of the damask) are best for scent. Heights vary to the maximum stated above.

VARIETIES Yellow: 'Whisky Mac', cupped blooms with 30 petals, very free flowering; 'Diorama', apricot with outer petals flushed pink; 'Grandmere Jenny', pale yellow flushed pink. Red: 'Alec's Red', cherry red, very full blooms; 'Ernest H. Morse', deep, brilliant red, beautifully shaped blooms; 'Wendy Cussons'; 'Papa Meilland'. Pink: 'Eden Rose', delicious fragrance, up to 60 deep pink petals; 'Blessings' *(above)*, coral pink, full blooms; 'Ophelia'; 'Prima Ballerina'. White: 'Message', greenish-white, full blooms; 'Tynwald', full, creamy bowl-shaped flowers, dark green foliage. Orange: 'Duke of Windsor', orange vermilion; 'Just Joey', coppery-orange; 'Sutter's Gold', light orange veined red. Multi: 'Shot Silk', pink-orange-gold.

## CLIMBING

| summer | hardy | semi-shade | 2.5m/8ft | 10m/30ft |
|--------|-------|------------|----------|----------|

All gardens need their fair share of climbing plants, both to clothe bare vertical surfaces and to add height to the overall design. There are few climbers as lavish as roses or with so much variety to offer. Some are true climbers, others sports of bush roses, all of varying parentage. The most vigorous usually derive from species roses, like *Rosa filipes* 'Kiftsgate', which can reach 18m/60ft, flowers once in mid-summer and is suitable for scrambling over trees. Walls, fences and archways need less vigorous varieties, derived from noisettes and large-flowered bush roses, and there are plenty to choose from. Climbing roses do not flower until they are well established.

VARIETIES Height and spread may vary to the maximum or more as stated above. Summer flowering: *R. f.* 'Kiftsgate', spectacular climber, numerous large clusters of very fragrant cream flowers; 'Mme Grégoire Staechelin' *(above)*, 6m/20ft, double, deep pink, good for shadier sites; 'Mrs Herbert Stevens', white tinged green, exquisite, pointed blooms; 'Maigold', 3m/10ft, double bronze-yellow, thorny. Continuous flowering: 'Zéphirine Drouhin', 4m/12ft bourbon, thornless, carmine pink; 'Guinee', 2.4m/8ft, intense deep red shaded black; 'Celine Forestier', 3m/10ft, tea-scented noisette, pale yellow; 'Gloire de Dijon', 5m/15ft, globe-shaped pendent blooms variously pink, salmon and yellow.

### ▓ PLANTING TIP

*Large-flowered roses are grafted on to vigorous root stocks. If shoots, known as suckers, start to grow up from the root stock, they will have a tendency to take over from the grafted, named variety. Suckers should be removed immediately by tearing them off where they emerge from the roots.*

### ▓ ORGANIC TIP

*Climbing roses need special attention if being trained to cover walls. Overhanging gables deprive them of rainfall and the heat reflected from walls in summer is considerable. Hot, dry conditions favour the spread of powdery mildew. If you do not want to spray, frequent watering keeps it at bay.*

## RAMBLING

| summer | hardy | full sun | 4m/12ft | 10m/30ft |

## MODERN SHRUB

| summer | hardy | full sun | 1.8m/6ft | 1.5m/5ft |

Rambling roses come from *Rosa luciae*, a species of Asian origin which bears tiny white flowers in clusters of up to 20. They are fragrant and followed by masses of purple-red hips. Subsequent crossings have been made with other species, but still a profusion of flowers and the suppleness of the stems characterize this group, which is very useful for training over unsightly but immovable features of the garden.

VARIETIES Height and spread may vary to the maximum or more as stated above. Once-flowering: 'Albertine' *(above)*, 6m/20ft, copper-pink; 'Félicité et Perpétue', 6m/20ft, creamy-white, dense growth – 'Abbandonata' is a pink form; 'Goldfinch', 4m/12ft, yellow fading to cream, highly scented; 'Bobbie James', 6m/20ft, abundant, white, musk-scented flowers. Repeat-flowering: 'Emily Gray', 3m/10ft, rich golden buff, almost evergreen (light pruning only); 'Thelma', 2.7m/9ft, pillar rose with clusters of soft coral pink flowers; 'Polyantha Grandiflora', 6m/20ft, trusses of fruity scented, white flowers; 'Veilchenblau' 5m/15ft, violet-blue with white centre, yellow stamens, strong grower, thornless; 'Sanders White', 4m/12ft, profusion of double white flowers.

It is not possible to trace the parentage of modern shrub roses, which have been created by highly skilled plant breeders to give an enormous variety. With the aim of adding the virtues of disease-resistance and repeat flowering to an inexhaustible choice of colour, scent is sometimes sacrificed. There are, however, some varieties in this most useful group which have it all. Included here are hybrid musk roses, shrubs raised in the early twentieth-century specifically for fragrance.

VARIETIES 'Golden Wings' *(above)*, 1.2m/4ft, single, pale yellow blooms with prominent stamens, pale green leaves; 'Lavender Lassie', 1.2m/4ft high and spreading, clusters of lavender-pink flowers; 'The Seckford Rose', 1.8m/6ft, good for hedging, double coral pink, beautifully cup-shaped flowers; 'Constance Spry', 2.1m/7ft, cup-shaped very large, deep pink flowers. Hybrid musks: 'Buff Beauty', 1.2m/4ft, apricot, double flowers; 'Cornelia', 1.2m/4ft, sprays of salmon pink blooms shaded apricot; 'Moonlight', 1.2 m/4ft, creamy white, very fragrant flowers with golden stamens, dark foliage; 'Penelope', sprays of highly scented, salmon-pink flowers fading to gold, good for hedging.

## ■ SPECIAL CARE TIP

*Most ramblers ('Albertine' is an exception) produce new canes at ground level yearly. To avoid congestion, cut back some of the old, flowered shoots in autumn.*

## ■ PLANTING TIP

*Modern shrubs roses, because of their mixed parentage, are very varied in habit. Choose carefully to find the right rose for your garden. For example,*

*you cannot confine exuberant shrubs like 'Nevada' and 'Penelope' in a small formal border without having to prune back all the flowering stems.*

# ENGLISH

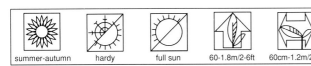

| | | | | |
|---|---|---|---|---|
| summer-autumn | hardy | full sun | 60-1.8m/2-6ft | 60cm-1.2m/2-4ft |

English roses make up a large and important category of modern shrub rose, almost all bred since 1970 and the work of a single rose breeder, David Austin. Unlike modern shrub roses in general, the emphasis is on producing roses with the repeat-flowering and wider colour range of large-flowered bush roses, while retaining the fragrance, subtlety of shade and, most importantly, the flower shape of old roses. Another important characteristic is the natural, bushy shape of these roses, together with a generally restrained habit that makes them ideal for smaller gardens. They can be left virtually unpruned, apart from the removal of weak or diseased wood, occasional cutting out of the oldest growth, and general heading back to improve shape, but the smaller types can also be pruned hard if space is at a premium. They make an excellent choice for mixed borders, rose beds or specimen plants.

VARIETIES There are dozens to choose from. Try 'Heritage', cup-shaped flowers in shell pink with a lemony-rose scent, reaching 1.2m/4ft; 'The Prince', crimson ageing to royal purple, very fragrant, just 60-75cm/24-30in tall; 'Graham Thomas' *(above)*, rich yellow with a tea-rose fragrance, 1.2m/4ft, 'Fair Bianca' pure white, similar to a damask rose, 90cm/3ft tall.

# MINIATURE

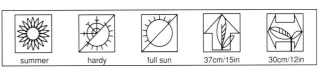

| | | | | |
|---|---|---|---|---|
| summer | hardy | full sun | 37cm/15in | 30cm/12in |

The parent of all true miniature roses is a variety of the China rose, *R. chinensis* syn. *R. indica*, properly *R. c.* 'Minima' but known as 'Rouletti' after the horticulturist who introduced it. Subsequent hybridization has produced a number of modern miniatures, which bear clusters of tiny flowers on little bushes. They are repeat-flowering, but unfortunately few are fragrant, with the exception of the half-dozen listed here. As miniature roses are best grown together, set about 25 cm/10 in apart in raised beds, this makes the scented varieties a good choice in gardens for the blind (and they are almost thornless).

VARIETIES 'Baby Faurax', violet-blue, semi-double blooms in large clusters, glossy light green foliage; 'Baby Gold Star', golden yellow, full blooms; 'Little Flirt' *(above)*, orange-red petals flushed yellow outside; 'Bo-Peep', deep rose pink; 'Diane', red double blooms, very free-flowering; 'Sweet Fairy', lilac-rose-pink. 'Little Gem' is a dwarf moss rose, not a true miniature, with very fragrant deep crimson blooms.

## SPECIAL CARE TIP

*Never plant roses on a site where roses have recently been grown. They fail to thrive due to the replant disorder, rose sickness. The only way around this is to replace the soil to a depth of some 60cm/2ft or sterilize the existing soil with formalin – not a task many gardeners would wish to undertake.*

## PLANTING TIP

*With the development of miniature roses, absolutely any garden can have its rose bed, even in a window box, but be attentive to feeding and watering.*

91

# SHRUBS

Some of the most important features to select and place in your garden are the permanent ones. Your choice will help provide the basic structure to your garden, for years to come.

In drawing up a planting plan for a garden there are many criteria to consider, particularly when selecting shrubs, but it is well worth adding perfume to your list. It can make the difference between a garden that is just pretty and one that is truly memorable, all year round.

**CHOOSING AND PLANTING** Soil requirements and position are more important when planting shrubs than for any other type of plant. You will want shrubs to remain in their position for many years, so make certain they will be happy and have the best possible

start. This may mean that you will have to exclude rhododendrons or other acid-loving shrubs from your chalky garden, but there are plenty of other good shrubs that will give better results than a sadly yellowing azalea, struggling for survival. Don't try and fight nature — work with it. There will be a shrub to suit your conditions, it's simply a question of finding it.

The main choice in shrubs is between deciduous and evergreen. Although evergreen add year-round structure to the garden, and are often the sole source of interest from late autumn through to spring, they tend to be less hardy than deciduous and they are rarely as spectacular in flowering, so a mix is essential.

The eventual height and spread of a shrub is another very important factor to consider, as well as its speed of growth. Moving an established shrub is a major undertaking, so it's worth taking the trouble to get it in the right position from the outset. Shrubs are available in containers for planting at any time of year, conditions permitting, and if the ground is waterlogged or frozen, they can be kept in their containers until the weather improves. The best times for planting evergreens, however, are mid-spring or early autumn, when the soil is warm enough to encourage root development but the weather unlikely to be too dry, thus reducing the very real risk of the plant drying out.

Because a shrub is intended to remain in its chosen position for a number of years, it is worth taking some trouble when you plant it. Ensure the ground is free of perennial weeds, then dig a hole wider than the root spread in the desired position. Fork the bottom of the hole to improve drainage and add well- rotted organic matter and bone meal as a base dressing to encourage root development. Position the shrub in the hole, then back-fill, firming as you do so to eradicate any air pockets.

Try to ensure that the shrub is at the same depth as in the nursery (for bare-rooted plants), or in the pot for container-grown specimens. If planted too shallowly, it is likely to suffer from wind rock which will damage the roots, if planted too deeply the stems may rot. In either case the plant is unlikely to survive.

**SHRUBS IN THE GARDEN** Shrubs vary tremendously in size and habit, and provide some of the hardiest, most versatile and useful plants you could ever wish for. They can be planted as specimens in a lawn, for example, either singly or in a group of identical cultivars, in special shrub borders, or in mixed borders where they provide the framework against which perennials, annuals and bulbs play their more fleeting roles.

There are so many elements to consider when choosing and positioning a shrub: foliage colour, shape and texture, the overall shape of the shrub, its flowers and, on top of all that, its scent.

Shrubs are one of the very few plants that offer a real opportunity of scent in the dead of winter, with such delicious offerings as *sarcococca*, or Christmas Box which, although not showy with its low suckering shoots of dark green, pointed leaves and tiny white flowers, has a delicious perfume that can spread over a large distance, and makes a neat evergreen background for *helleborus niger*, or the Christmas rose. *daphne mezereum* is another shrub whose perfume can bring passers-by to a standstill, even on the other side of a hedge, while they try and guess the source of such a scent in early spring, although for the rest of the year, it is quite modest looking.

There are huge numbers of scented shrubs to choose from for the rest of the year, from tiny, front-of-border specimens, to large imposing plants that would dominate the average modern garden. In between are the many good, reliable, average-sized shrubs that are quite at home in mixed borders.

**MAINTAINING THE SHRUB BORDER** Once a shrub is planted in a suitable position, it will require very little further maintenance, beyond regular watering, particularly in the first couple of years, a yearly top-dressing of fertilizer in spring, and pruning where appropriate to enhance flowering or improve shape. This makes shrubs an ideal choice for a gardener with limited time to spare. Nonetheless, results will be

*As long as conditions are right, acid, peaty soil with dappled shade and shelter from frosts, azaleas will give a most enchanting display of vivid colour from mid- to late spring.*

much better if you resolve to keep an eye on your shrubs and take care of problems as soon as they arise.

Look out for signs of pests and diseases, such as discoloured foliage or bark, premature leaf-fall, damaged or distorted shoots, or general lack of vigour. Dealt with promptly, by cutting back and/or spraying, such outbreaks can usually be contained but the speed at which, for example, a fungus disease or aphid infestation can spread through the garden is truly alarming and can result in the loss of prize specimens.

Check over shrubs after strong winds, heavy rain or hail, and falls of snow. Evergreens in particular can loose whole branches, torn off by the weight of an overnight snow fall, and hedges can be ruined if snow or ice are not brushed off the branches as soon as possible. Branches torn or damaged by wind or rain present an ideal entry point for fungal spores or other disease-causing organisms. Cut them back cleanly into healthy wood as soon as possible.

Finally, although perennial weeds will, of course, have been dug up or sprayed off prior to planting a shrub, they have a nasty habit of returning and will compete with the roots of your shrub for water and nutrients. A systemic weedkiller in gel form can be painted onto the leaves of perennial weeds without danger to nearby cultivated plants. The weed problem is one you really must stay on top of, or it will soon overwhelm you.

93

# HOHERIA

| summer | half hardy | full sun | 4.5m/15ft | 3m/10ft |

Hoherias are native to New Zealand (the name comes from a Maori word) and, like hollyhocks and hibiscus, belong to the mallow family. Not all species are hardy in temperate zones, but one of the deciduous types which bears scented flowers will survive most winters in warmer districts. This is the exquisite *H. lyallii (above)*, with abundant clusters of pure white, funnel-shaped flowers with numerous yellow stamens. The foliage is dull green and slightly downy.

**PROPAGATION AND GROWING** Plant in spring on any good, well-drained soil. Choose a position in sun or light shade, protected from cold winds. Hoherias thrive against sunny walls. Propagate by layering. Prune to remove damaged wood in spring.

**VARIETIES** *H. l. glabra*, similar to the species but with smooth leaves, cup-shaped flowers.

**POSSIBLE PROBLEMS** Generally trouble-free.

# VIBURNUM

| spring | hardy | full sun | 1.8m/6ft | 2.4m/8ft |

The genus Viburnum includes 200 species, many of them highly esteemed garden plants, many fragrant. Some flower in winter before the leaves appear, some in spring and early summer. Blooms are usually white or pink.

**PROPAGATION AND GROWING** Plant from autumn to spring (deciduous species), in autumn or spring (evergreens), on any moist, fertile soil in a sheltered, sunny position. Propagate from cuttings in summer or by layering. Thin old and damaged stems in spring (evergreens) or after flowering.

**VARIETIES** *V. juddii* , pink or white flowers, dark green leaves; *V. opulus* (guelder rose), up to 5m/15ft, flat heads of white flowers in spring; *V. fragrans*, 4m/12ft, clusters of pink-white flowers in winter; *V. × burkwoodii (above)*, evergreen, 2.4m/8ft, dark green leaves, dense heads of waxy white flowers in spring.

**POSSIBLE PROBLEMS** Aphids; honey fungus; frost damage.

## ▮ PROPAGATION TIP

*Hoheria can be grown from seed, but the young plants go through a juvenile stage during which they have a dense, twiggy shape and small leaves of a different shape from those of the mature plant. This can be a surprise if you are not expecting it. Propagation by cuttings or layering does not give this result.*

## ▮ PLANTING TIP

*For truly spectacular fragrance from late autumn until early spring, plant V. × bodnantense 'Dawn', a deciduous hybrid. The flower buds start to open from the time the leaves fall and continue, particularly in mild periods. It does well in a clay soil.*

# Rhododendron

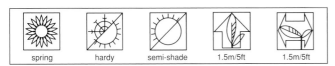

| spring | hardy | semi-shade | 1.5m/5ft | 1.5m/5ft |

# Carpenteria

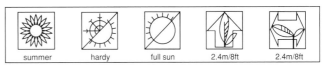

| summer | hardy | full sun | 2.4m/8ft | 2.4m/8ft |

Rhododendrons are second only to roses in popularity. Scented flowers are borne by some species and a number of hardy hybrids from various crossings, most of which bear pink or white trumpet-shaped flowers in dense clusters. Loderi hybrids extend the colour range.

**PROPAGATION AND GROWING** Rhododendrons are shallow-rooting, and hate lime. Set out young plants in early autumn in well-drained, moisture-retentive acid soil. Light shade is best, but full sun is tolerated. Remove faded flower-heads. Prune lightly in spring, if necessary, to restrict growth. Propagate species by layering, hybrids from cuttings.

**VARIETIES** (evergreens) *R. auriculatum*, 6m/20ft, late-flowering, white flowers flushed pink; *R. bullatum*, 1.8m/6ft, half-hardy, waxy white-pink flowers; *R. crassum*, 4.5m/15ft, half-hardy, white flowers in summer; *R. decorum*, 3m/10ft, very hardy, pale pink or white flowers; *R. fortunei*, very hardy, 3.6m/12ft, pale pink. Hybrids: 'Mount Everest' *(above)*, 4.5m/15ft, white with small red blotch; Loderi group: 'May Day', 1.5m/5ft, scarlet; 'Temple Bells', 1.5m/5ft, lilac; 'Vanessa', 1.5m/5ft, rich pink.

**POSSIBLE PROBLEMS** Rhododendron leaf hopper.

*Carpenteria californica (above)*, as its name suggests, is a native of the west coast of America and thrives in a warm climate. In cooler zones this evergreen needs the protection of a sunny wall. Like its cousin the mock orange, this shrub bears sweetly fragrant white flowers with showy yellow stamens. The glossy mid-green leaves, white-felted beneath, are long and narrow.

**PROPAGATION AND GROWING** Plant container-grown specimens in spring in any type of well-drained fertile soil in a sunny, sheltered situation. Carpenterias are lime-tolerant. Remove old or damaged wood from mature specimens, if necessary, after flowering. New plants may be raised from seed, by layering or, with difficulty, from cuttings taken in early summer.

**VARIETIES** There are no named varieties.

**POSSIBLE PROBLEMS** Generally trouble-free.

■ SPECIAL CARE TIP

When removing faded flowerheads to prevent seed production, avoid using secateurs which could damage immature buds. Remove by hand instead.

■ SPECIAL CARE TIP

Carpenteria *can fail to flower in cold climates or in exposed positions. It needs plenty of sun to ripen the flowering wood. Bear this in mind when siting slightly* tender shrubs. A combination of both shelter and sunshine is often needed.

# SYRINGA

| spring | hardy | full sun | 3m/10ft | 3m/10ft |

The scent of lilacs is unique, one of the few against which others can be measured. Most, but not all, types are fragrant and all flower in late spring, bearing panicles of lilac, blue, pink, purple or white flowers, which may be double. The fresh green leaves are oval-pointed in shape. Shrubby lilacs may be grown as specimens, in borders, or for screening.

**PROPAGATION AND GROWING** Plant in late autumn in a rich, moist, loamy soil. Remove most of the first year's flowers to build up strength, and in subsequent years remove the flowers as soon as they have faded. Always pull away any suckering growths from the stem. Propagate from cuttings.

**VARIETIES** Extremely fragrant are: S. × *chinensis* (Rouen lilac), an abundance of lilac flowers; S. × *c. alba (above)*, white; S. × *c. duplex*, purple, double. *S. persica*, (Persian lilac), up to 2m/7ft, fluffy lilac panicles. 'Ethel M. Webster' (Canadian hybrid), 20cm/8in pale pink panicles. *S. vulgaris* (common lilac) varieties include 'Katherine Havemeyer', large purple trusses; 'Souvenir de Louis Spath', rich reddish-purple; 'Mme Charles Souchet', pale blue, early flowering; 'Ellen Willmott', large, double pure white trusses.

**POSSIBLE PROBLEMS** Die back if grafted on to privet rootstock; frost damage; lilac blight.

# OLEARIA

| summer | half-hardy | full sun | 2.4m/8ft | 2.1m/7ft |

One look at the broad clusters of flowers adorning O. *macrodonta (above)* in early summer and it is obvious why the common name is daisy bush. The blooms are musk-scented, and well-set off by holly-like glossy green leaves. This slow-growing evergreen does best in warm districts and thrives in seaside gardens.

**PROPAGATION AND GROWING** Plant in spring in any type of well-drained soil, in full sun. Propagate by cuttings taken in late summer. Prune to shape in spring if necessary.

**VARIETIES** O. *ilicifolia* (Maori holly), sharply toothed leaves, smaller flower clusters.

**POSSIBLE PROBLEMS** Generally trouble-free.

## ▇ SPECIAL CARE TIP

*Leggy, neglected lilacs can be cut back in winter to about 30cm/12in from the ground. Fed and mulched well, they will flower after two or three years.*

## ▇ PLANTING TIP

*The foliage of* olearia *is very decorative and useful in flower arranging, as the underside of the leaves is a felty, matt white. It tolerates hard pruning.*

# CHOISYA

| spring | hardy | full sun | 1.8m/6ft | 1.8m/6ft |

# DEUTZIA

| summer | hardy | semi-shade | 1.2m/4ft | 1.8m/6ft |

*Choisya ternata* or Mexican orange blossom *(above)* is an evergreen shrub with glossy fan-shaped leaves that provide a focal point in an otherwise bereft winter border. When crushed they give out a pungent, peppery aroma, in contrast to the sweetness of the white flowers which appear in spring.

**PROPAGATION AND GROWING** Plant in spring on any type of well-drained garden soil. A sunny spot is best, though light shade is tolerated. As the plant is vulnerable to frost, in cold districts it is best sited against a warm sunny wall. Any frost-damaged shoots should be removed in spring, but otherwise little pruning is needed. In temperate zones choisya is unlikely to exceed 1.5 x 1.5m/5 x 5ft.

**VARIETIES** 'Sundance', slow-growing to 1m/3ft, bright golden foliage.

**POSSIBLE PROBLEMS** Honey fungus.

Although they belong to the Philadelphus (mock orange) family, deutzias do not rival their popular relative in sweetness of perfume. The scent of some deutzias is hawthorn-like, a quality which will not appeal to everyone; others can certainly be described as fragrant. All are highly decorative, handsome plants, covered with star-shaped flowers of pink, purple or white in summer. The bark eventually peels away from the stems to give added interest.

**PROPAGATION AND GROWING** Plant from autumn to early spring in any type of well-cultivated soil. Full sun is tolerated but may bleach the flowers; dappled shade is preferable, in a sheltered position. Cut back flowering stems as soon as the flowers have faded. Propagate by cuttings taken in summer.

**VARIETIES** *D. gracilis (above)*, panicles of pure white flowers, often grown in pots and brought indoors in late winter for early flowering. *D. g. aurea* is a yellow variety. *D. compacta*, hawthorn-scented, but fresh, with clusters of cream flowers; *D. c.* 'Lavender Time' bears lilac flowers that deepen in colour as they age. *D. corymbosa*, up to 2.7m/9ft high, white, hawthorn-scented flowers; *D. sieboldiana*, heart-shaped leaves, panicles of honey-scented white flowers.

**POSSIBLE PROBLEMS** Sensitive to spring frosts in exposed positions.

## PROPAGATION TIP

*If no frost-free position is available for this lovely shrub, it can be grown in a large container and moved into shelter during the winter.*

## PLANTING TIP

*The positioning of deutzias in the garden can be tricky in colder areas. If given too much shelter, their leaves and flower buds appear earlier than is desirable in spring, making them vulnerable to damage from late spring frosts, especially after a mild winter.*

# DAPHNE

| spring | hardy | sun | 1.5m/5ft 1.2m/4ft | 90cm/3ft 1.2m/4ft |
|--------|-------|-----|-------------------|--------------------|

All species of daphne have deliciously scented flowers and all, in their different ways, are highly decorative. Some are small enough for the rock garden. Some are evergreen, such as *D. laureola* and *D. pontica*, which are especially fragrant at night.

**PROPAGATION AND GROWING** Plant in autumn or spring in any well-drained soil (daphnes are lime-tolerant) in sun or partial shade. No pruning is necessary, unless to improve the shape in spring. Propagate by cuttings taken in summer.

**VARIETIES** *D. mezereum*, deciduous, with clusters of bright mauve-pink flowers which appear on leafless stems of an upright bush in very early spring, followed by scarlet berries; *D. × burkwoodii (above)*, semi-evergreen hybrid, clusters of pale pink flowers in early summer; *D. blagayana*, prostrate evergreen species up to 1.8m/6ft across, a few rounded leaves on long shoots with a mass of creamy-white flowers at the tip. Likes some shade, but no lime in the soil.

**POSSIBLE PROBLEMS** Aphids; cucumber mosaic virus.

# DIPELTA

| summer | hardy | semi-shade | 4.5m/15ft | 3m. 10ft |
|--------|-------|------------|-----------|----------|

The delicacy of its late spring blossom and the beauty of its light gold peeling bark give away dipelta's oriental origins. The flowers are trumpet-shaped, sugar pink and in one species very sweetly scented. The branches are useful in flower arrangements. This deciduous shrub has an upright, open shape and should be situated in a sheltered position, preferably against a wall.

**PROPAGATION AND GROWING** Plant in autumn or spring in any type of garden soil in semi-shade. Prune after flowering to keep the shape balanced, cutting a few old stems right back. Propagate from cuttings taken in summer, or hardwood cuttings in the autumn.

**VARIETIES** *D. floribunda (above)*, clusters of fragrant pale pink flowers flushed yellow, mid-green pointed leaves, distinctly veined, can be grown on shallow chalky soil; *D. yunnanensis*, non-scented species of graceful appearance, with cream flowers flushed pink.

**POSSIBLE PROBLEMS** Generally trouble-free.

---

■ SPECIAL CARE TIP

*All* daphnes *resent root disturbance, so cuttings should be rooted in pots and planted out young. A number of the species, notably* D. mezereum *and* D. laureola, *have poisonous berries, so great care should be taken about planting them in a garden frequented by children or animals.*

■ PLANTING TIP

*The flowers of these large shrubs are similar to those of* deutzia, *and are an excellent choice for the back of a shrub or mixed border, where they can benefit from the shelter they need to flower successfully.*

# OSMANTHUS

| spring/autumn | hardy | semi-shade | 1.5m/5ft | 1.5m/5ft |

All species of osmanthus are deliciously fragrant. Evergreens native to China, they are free-flowering, slow-growing shrubs that make a dense, attractively rounded bush in maturity. They may take 20 years to reach their ultimate size. Two species and a hybrid are recommended, bearing clusters of tiny but heavily scented white flowers at different times of year. One is good for hedging, if you are prepared to sacrifice most of the flowers.

**PROPAGATION AND GROWING** Plant between autumn and spring in well-drained soil in sun or partial shade in a sheltered position. No pruning is necessary. For hedging, set young plants 45cm/18in apart. Clip hedges in spring.

**VARIETIES** *O. delavayi (above)*, glossy box-like leaves, spring-flowering, and can be used in a mixed border; *O. heterophyllus* syns. *O. aquifolium, O.ilicifolius*, up to 3m/10ft, holly-like leaves, autumn-flowering, can be used for hedging; *O. × burkwoodii* syn. *× Osmaria burkwoodii*, 1.8 x 1.8m /6 x 6ft, masses of flowers in spring.

**POSSIBLE PROBLEMS** Generally trouble-free.

# BUDDLEIA

| summer | hardy | full sun | 4.5m/15ft | 3m/10ft |

Commonly known as butterfly bush, all species of buddleia have a powerful fragrance. Set it among other butterfly-attracting species, like *Sedum spectabile* and early michaelmas daisies, and at least one corner of the garden will be a-flutter in late summer. Buddleias are large, informal, deciduous shrubs with long tapering leaves and panicles of pink, purple or white flowers. Fast-growing, they look better for being pruned back in spring.

**PROPAGATION AND GROWING** Plant between autumn and spring on any well-drained soil in full sun.

**VARIETIES** *B. davidii*, likes a chalky soil, honey-scented; 'Black Knight', deep violet flowers, keeps its scent even when dried for flower arrangements; 'Harlequin', crimson flowers, variegated foliage; 'Peace', white flowers. *B. fallowiana*, narrow, greyish foliage, scented lavender flowers in late summer/early autumn. Neat at 2.4 x 1.8m/8 x 6ft; 'Lochinch', violet-blue; 'Alba' *(above)*, white.

**POSSIBLE PROBLEMS** Generally trouble-free.

## ▦ PLANTING TIP

*For more decorative interest, choose one of the varieties of O. heterophyllus with white, yellow or silver variegation on the leaves.*

## ▦ SPECIAL CARE TIP

B. davidii *is the species that benefits from hard pruning in early spring. Cut down to just a few buds from the ground, if you want, to keep it compact and bushy.*

*As it flowers on wood formed in the current season, it will develop its flowering wood after pruning.*

# DATURA

summer | half-hardy | full sun | 2.4m/8ft | 2.4m/8ft

Shrubby species of datura are often listed as Brugmansia. The one described here, *D. cornigera* syn. *Brugmansia knightii (above)*, is often known as angel's trumpet, an apt acknowledgement of its huge, creamy-white flowers. The double blooms are heavily fragrant and appear throughout the summer. As a native of Mexico, this magnificent shrub likes warmth, and does best in a greenhouse. Pot-grown specimens can be transferred outside in summer; in favoured localities they can be left outdoors permanently.

**PROPAGATION AND GROWING** Grow in pots or tubs of a loam-based compost, potting on annually in spring to a maximum container size of 30cm/12in. Prune hard each spring, and feed with liquid fertilizer every two weeks from repotting until flowering has ceased.

**VARIETIES** There are no named varieties.

**POSSIBLE PROBLEMS** Under glass, red spider mites may infest the leaves.

# MAHONIA

winter | hardy | full sun | 3m/10ft | 2.4m/8ft

All the mahonias bear numerous fragrant bright yellow flowers in winter or very early spring. This alone is enough to recommend them, but their other qualities – handsome evergreen foliage, and an accommodating disposition – make mahonias invaluable plants.

**PROPAGATION AND GROWING** Set out young plants in autumn or spring in fertile, well-drained soil which is not markedly alkaline. A situation in sun or partial shade will suit. Pruning is not usually necessary, except for *M. aquifolium* if grown as ground cover. Propagate by tip cuttings taken in summer.

**VARIETIES** *M.* × 'Charity' ; hybrid bearing erect 30cm/12in racemes of rich yellow flowers in mid-winter; *M. aquifolium*, called the Oregon grape after the blue-black berries which follow dense clusters of yellow flowers in spring, good for ground cover; *M. a. atropurpurea*, variety with rich red foliage in autumn. *M. japonica (above)*, winter-flowering, lemon-yellow blooms with a scent of lily-of-the-valley.

**POSSIBLE PROBLEMS** Leaf spot; powdery mildew.

## ORGANIC TIP

*Red spider mite is a very destructive pest that mainly affects plants grown under glass. It thrives in hot, dry conditions and can spread rapidly. It is difficult to control with chemicals. Under glass, biological control can be used by introducing its natural predator, a mite called Phytoseiulus.*

## PLANTING TIP

*Although M. × 'Charity' is suitable only for larger gardens, M. aquifolium makes an attractive feature all year round in a small mixed border.*

# CORYLOPSIS

| spring | hardy | full sun | 2.1m/7ft | 1.8m/6ft |

Corylopsis are members of the witch hazel family, and, like many spring-flowering shrubs, bear yellow flowers. The flowers of all species are fragrant; an added bonus is the attractive colour of the autumn foliage.

**PROPAGATION AND GROWING**  Plant from autumn to spring. Corylopsis are easy to grow on any type of lime-free soil, and appreciate some protection from frost, as they are one of the earliest shrubs to flower. The only pruning necessary is to remove old or weak wood after flowering. Propagate by layering.

**VARIETIES**  *C. willmottiae (above)*, 7.5cm/3in racemes of primrose-yellow flowers in early spring; *C. platypetala*, purple shoots precede creamy-yellow flowers; *C. spicata*, up to 1.8m/6ft high, small-cowslip-scented flowers, blue-green heart-shaped leaves.

**POSSIBLE PROBLEMS**  Generally trouble-free.

# STACHYURUS

| spring | hardy | full sun | 3m/10ft | 2.4m/8ft |

There are two species of stachyurus commonly available, both oriental in origin and both flowering in very early spring. Like many spring-flowering shrubs, they bear yellow flowers, which are lightly scented. They form racemes 10cm/4in long which hang unopened on the leafless branches all through the winter. The mid-green leaves, when they appear, are narrow and pointed and the shrub has an attractively graceful shape. Small greenish yellow berries succeed the flowers.

**PROPAGATION AND GROWING**  Plant between autumn and spring in peaty soil in full sun. Choose a site protected from cold winds. Pruning is not necessary. Propagate from cuttings taken in summer.

**VARIETIES**  *S. praecox (above)*, pale yellow flowers surrounded by red calyces; *S. chinensis*, very pale yellow flowers.

**POSSIBLE PROBLEMS**  Generally trouble-free.

## ▩ PLANTING TIP

*Try planting* C. sinensis *'Spring Purple', similar to* C. willmottiae, *but with the added decorative attraction of a blueish-purple tinge to the young leaves.*

## ▩ PROPAGATION TIP

*To improve the rooting of cuttings taken in late summer, provide some base heat. Another possible method is layering in spring.*

## SARCOCOCCA

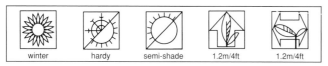

| winter | hardy | semi-shade | 1.2m/4ft | 1.2m/4ft |

Christmas box is an invaluable evergreen shrub for shade. The scent of the flowers spreads through the garden on a still mild day. All species are slow-growing with glossy foliage, useful in borders and to fill a dull corner. They even thrive beneath trees. Tiny, intensely fragrant white flowers appear in mid-winter and persist until the spring. They are followed by shiny black berries.

**PROPAGATION AND GROWING** Sarcococca species like fertile, humus-rich soil and succeed on chalk. Plant in autumn or spring. This is the ultimate no-maintenance plant – no after care is required. Propagate from rooted suckers.

**VARIETIES** *S. confusa* dense growth suitable for hedging; *S. humilis (above)*, only 45cm/18in high at most, excellent evergreen ground cover.

**POSSIBLE PROBLEMS** None.

## MYRTUS

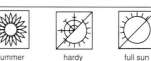  

| summer | hardy | full sun | 2.4m/8ft | 2.4m/8ft |

All species of myrtle are fragrant, but only one of these hand-some evergreens is hardy enough to thrive outdoors in temperate zones. This is *M. communis (above)*, a dense, leafy shrub which may exceed the height given if grown against a warm, sunny wall. The small, oval-pointed leaves are lustrous dark green and aromatic when bruised. Fragrant white flowers with numerous stamens appear in mid-summer, followed by round, purple fruits.

**PROPAGATION AND GROWING** Plant in spring in any type of well-drained soil in a sunny sheltered position. Prune annually in spring if necessary to improve the shape. Propagate by layering. Myrtle may be grown as a greenhouse pot plant, reaching about 90cm/3ft, which can be set outside in summer to scent a sheltered patio.

**VARIETIES** *M. c. leucocarpa*, as the species but with white fruits; *M. variegata*, leaves variegated creamy-white.

**POSSIBLE PROBLEMS** Leaf spot.

---

### ▦ PLANTING TIP

*This is a useful shrub for flower arrangers, who will combine it with forsythia or winter-flowering jasmine for a fragrant, late-winter display. As it is a rather* *slow-growing shrub, however, it may be advisable to plant several specimens to provide sufficient plant material for cutting.*

### ▦ PROPAGATION TIP

*Myrtle can also be propagated from heel cuttings taken in summer. Its fragrant flowers and foliage make it popular in flower arranging,* *particularly for weddings, and plants raised from the material used in the bouquet were traditionally given to the bride for sentimental value.*

**SHRUBS**

102

# PHILADELPHUS

|  |  |  |  |  |
|---|---|---|---|---|
| summer | hardy | full sun | 8m/6ft | 1.5m/5ft |

Philadelphus flowers have an intoxicating, fruity scent, giving rise to the popular name mock orange. All species bear an abundance of white flowers in early to mid-summer. These imposing shrubs (many species exceed the given height) combine well with roses or with perennials in a mixed border. They also make excellent specimens in a large lawn.

**PROPAGATION AND GROWING** Plant between autumn and spring in any type of well-drained soil, including chalky soils, in sun or light shade. Give a mulch of well-rotted compost from time to time. Prune as soon as the flowers have faded, thinning out older wood from the base. Propagate by cuttings taken in summer.

**VARIETIES** *P. × lemoinei*, hybrid with upright habit of growth useful in mixed borders, pure white flowers; 'Avalanche', 'Innocence' and 'Norma' (3m/10ft), single-flowered varieties; 'Manteau d'Hermine', 'Enchantment' and 'Virginal' double-flowered. *P. coronarius*, spreading, rounded bush, creamy-white flowers; *P. c. aureus (above)*, bright yellow leaves; *P. c. dianthiflorus*, double flowers.

**POSSIBLE PROBLEMS** Leaf spot.

# MAGNOLIA

|  |  |  |  | |
|---|---|---|---|---|
| summer | hardy | full sun | 5m/15ft | 3m/10ft |

There are numerous fragrant magnolias for different situations; they often take several years after first planting to bear flowers. *M. grandiflora (above)* is an evergreen tree commonly grown as a wall shrub, where it may well exceed the height given above. Throughout the summer it bears lemon-scented cup-shaped cream flowers up to 20cm/8in across. The waxy blooms are offset by large, glossy dark green leaves. Grown in the open this species makes a magnificent round-headed tree.

**PROPAGATION AND GROWING** Plant in spring in fertile, well-drained soil in a sheltered site. Provide stakes to support young plants. Top-dress with well-rotted compost or peat every spring. Pruning is only required if *M. grandiflora* is grown against a wall: in spring, remove shoots which are facing outwards from the base.

**VARIETIES** (all spring-flowering) *M. × loebneri*, hybrid, 3m/10ft, narrow-petalled white flowers even on young plants; *M. salicifolia*, 6m/20ft, slender white flowers with orange-blossom scent appear before the aromatic foliage; *M. sprengeri diva*, large tree with huge chalice-shaped carmine-pink flowers, heavily scented.

**POSSIBLE PROBLEMS** Frost damage to spring-flowering species; leaf spot.

---

## ▒ SPECIAL CARE TIP

*Compact varieties of mock orange that do not exceed 1.2m/4ft in height, such as P. × 'Beauclerk', are available, and are suitable for small gardens. If left unpruned, large varieties soon become leggy, only producing flowers and foliage high up, with unattractive bare branches at eye level.*

## ▒ SPECIAL CARE TIP

*M. × loebneri is more tolerant of lime than many magnolias, which can be disappointing if not given their ideal neutral to acid, humus-rich soil.*

# CYTISUS

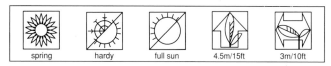

| | | | | |
|---|---|---|---|---|
| spring | hardy | full sun | 4.5m/15ft | 3m/10ft |

Cytisus, spartium and genista are closely related types of broom belonging to the pea family. Like its cousins, cytisus loves the sun but bears a profusion of yellow flowers in late spring rather than the height of summer. Not all species are sweetly scented; in fact, some would describe the odour of the Warminster broom, C. × praecox, as acrid.

**PROPAGATION AND GROWING** Set out container-grown plants in autumn or spring, in light, well-drained soil in a sunny position. Lime in the soil is tolerated, but is likely to limit the plant's life expectancy. Raise new plants from seed.

**VARIETIES** C. battandieri (above), silvery foliage, large, yellow pineapple-scented, pineapple-shaped flowers, does well against a wall.

**POSSIBLE PROBLEMS** Generally trouble-free.

# SANTOLINA

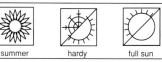 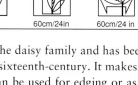

| | | | | |
|---|---|---|---|---|
| summer | hardy | full sun | 60cm/24in | 60cm/24 in |

Cotton lavender is a member of the daisy family and has been a popular garden plant since the sixteenth-century. It makes a low, dense rounded shrub and can be used for edging or as a low hedge. The refreshing scent is in the feathery, silver-grey leaves rather than the button-like, yellow flowers which appear in profusion in mid-summer. These hardy evergreens are sun-lovers from the Mediterranean, and clumps may become patchy in prolonged wet weather or in severe winters.

**PROPAGATION AND GROWING** Plant in autumn or spring in full sun on well-drained, sandy soil, spacing plants at 37cm/15in intervals for hedging. Pinch out the growing tips occasionally until established. Remove flowerheads as they fade. Trim hedges lightly in summer. Prune all bushes hard in spring to encourage new growth from the base. Propagate from cuttings.

**VARIETIES** S. chamaecyparissus, acid lemon flowers, woolly foliage; S. incana, dwarf species for rock gardens; S. neapolitana syn. S. rosmarinifolia (above), bright yellow flowerheads on slender erect stalks, white-felted foliage.

**POSSIBLE PROBLEMS** Generally trouble-free.

■ SPECIAL CARE TIP

*Although not sweetly scented, C. × praecox is the hardiest variety, and is therefore the most commonly grown in cooler climates. It can even be used as an informal hedge, but since it flowers on wood formed the previous year, like most cytisus, it should be pruned straight after flowering.*

■ SPECIAL CARE TIP

*If santolina is grown as a formal hedge, it is very important to cut it back hard in mid-spring. It will need to be replaced every 5 or 6 years, but that provides the opportunity to dig out any perennial weeds that have grown into the base of the plants, which are almost impossible to eradicate otherwise.*

# ELAEAGNUS

|  |  |  |  |  |
|:--:|:--:|:--:|:--:|:--:|
| autumn | hardy | semi-shade | 3.6m/12ft | 3.6m/12ft |

Elaeagnus includes both evergreen and deciduous species, flowering at different times. Some bear fruits from which an edible jelly can be made, some have beautiful silver foliage. All are fragrant to some degree. They are fast-growing and very accommodating as to soil and situation. Evergreen species make good hedging plants and do well in seaside gardens.

**PROPAGATION AND GROWING** Deciduous: plant in late autumn in full sun. Propagate from seed sown in summer. Evergreen: plant in spring or early autumn in sun or semi-shade. For hedging, set young plants 45cm/18in apart, more for screens, and cut back by one third after planting. Propagate from cuttings taken in summer.

**VARIETIES** *E. angustifolia* (oleaster), deciduous, thrives in sandy soil, mature height 4.5m/15ft, exquisite willow-like silvery leaves, white flowers in summer, followed by dark gold edible fruits. The following evergreens are good for hedging: *E. pungens* , glossy oval leaves, silver underneath, and aromatic in some varieties; white flowers in autumn followed by orange fruits; *E. p.* 'Marginata' *(above)*; *E. p. aureo-variegata*, variety with leaves splashed brilliant yellow; *E. p. tricolor*, leaves green, yellow and pale pink. *E. × ebbingei*, vigorous grower, oval, leaves, white flowers in autumn, orange fruits.

**POSSIBLE PROBLEMS** Leaf spot.

# SPARTIUM

|  |  |  |  | |
|:--:|:--:|:--:|:--:|:--:|
| summer | hardy | full sun | 3m/10ft | 2.4m/8ft |

*Spartium junceum* or Spanish broom *(above)* is a member of the pea family related to *Genista hispanica* or Spanish gorse *(see page 107)*, which it closely resembles, except in size. Its bright green stems bear few leaves, and these soon drop. Golden yellow, fragrant flowers bloom all summer. This is a good plant for seaside gardens, as it withstands strong winds.

**PROPAGATION AND GROWING** Plant in autumn or spring on well-drained soil. Sun is essential; the plant is not fully hardy in severe winters. To keep it as shapely as possible – given that broom has a spreading habit – shorten the previous year's growth each spring, cutting the stems right back. Dead-head to prevent seeding.

**VARIETIES** *S. j. ochroleuceum*, creamy-white flowers.

**POSSIBLE PROBLEMS** Generally trouble-free.

## ▨ SPECIAL CARE TIP

Elaeagnus, *particularly the evergreen varieties, are great favourites with flower arrangers. Their stiff, gracefully curved branches make excellent* *line material. Even more important, they are quite happy to be cut back to provide foliage, but take care not to spoil the shape.*

## ▨ PLANTING TIP

*The honey scented, long-lived flowers of* spartium *make it ideal for planting in a sunny spot outside a window or by a sheltered patio.*

# Hamamelis

| winter | hardy | full sun | 2.4m/8ft | 2.4m/8ft |

# Chimonanthus

| winter | hardy | full sun | 3m/10ft | 2.4m/8ft |

Witch hazels bear their sweetly scented, spidery flowers in winter when the slender branches are still bare of leaves (they can be cut and used in long-lasting flower arrangements). There is another pleasure in store, as the foliage takes on brilliant tones of red, yellow and orange in autumn. Witch hazels make excellent specimen trees, but also combine well with perennials and bulbs in a mixed border or island bed.

**PROPAGATION AND GROWING** Plant between autumn and spring in slightly acid, moisture-retentive soil on a site sheltered from cold winds. Prune established specimens after flowering, cut back straggly growth. Propagate by layering.

**VARIETIES** *H. mollis* or Chinese witch hazel *(above)*, golden yellow flowers flushed red clothe the stems in mid-winter, foliage yellow in autumn; 'Pallida', variety with numerous, paler flowers; *H. vernalis*, an American species, dense shrub reaching up to 1.8m/6ft, one of the earliest to flower, good waterside plant.

**POSSIBLE PROBLEMS** Generally trouble-free.

*Chimonanthus praecox (above)*, the winter sweet, bears its yellow and purple flowers on leafless branches in mid-winter. They have a rich, spicy scent – indeed all parts of the shrub are fragrant to some degree. The branches are useful for indoor flower arrangements. Place chimonanthus in a sheltered sunny site or against a wall where the scent may drift into the house. To conceal the naked branches in summer, let a climber, such as clematis or passiflora, scramble over them.

**PROPAGATION AND GROWING** Plant from autumn to spring on any type of well-cultivated soil, in full sun. Prune wall-trained specimens in spring, cutting flowered shoots right back; simply remove weak or damaged stems from shrubs grown in the open. Propagate by layering; plants take up to seven years to reach flowering size.

**VARIETIES** 'Grandiflorus', has large yellow flowers with red centres, it is very eye-catching but less fragrant; 'Lutens', clear yellow flowers.

**POSSIBLE PROBLEMS** Generally trouble-free.

■ PLANTING TIP

*Although* hamamelis *is best placed near a path or close to the house where its scent will be appreciated even on the coldest days, it is not of great interest in summer. Make sure you place some attractive, summer-flowering plants nearby, to take over from it later in the year.*

■ PLANTING TIP

*Although very fragrant at a time when there is little interest in the garden, chimonanthus is a poor choice for a small garden, since its season of interest is so short, and a sudden frost can wipe out all the flowers. For a similar effect, but less risk, plant hamamelis or witch hazel.*

# GENISTA

| summer | hardy | full sun | 90cm/3ft | 2.1m/7ft |

All the brooms bear a profusion of yellow flowers which by their shape identify them as members of the pea family. Two are fragrant and make fine specimens.

**PROPAGATION AND GROWING** Set out young plants in spring in light, well-drained soil. Full sun is essential. Feeding and mulching is not advisable. Pinch out the growing points after flowering to keep a bushy shape. Propagate by cuttings taken in late summer.

**VARIETIES** *G. hispanica* (Spanish gorse) in early summer the needle-like leaves are overwhelmed by a mass of brilliant yellow flowers with a fruity scent, plants become leggy with age; *G. aetnensis* or Mt. Etna broom *(above)*, fast-growing to 3m/10ft or more, golden yellow flowers in late summer, emitting a scent of vanilla. Cut back several times when young. Heavy branches of mature plants may need support.

**POSSIBLE PROBLEMS** Generally trouble-free.

# FOTHERGILLA

| spring | hardy | full sun | 2.4m/8ft | 1.8m/6ft |

Fothergillas are slow-growing deciduous shrubs belonging to the witch hazel family. All species bear cream, sweetly scented flowers in spring when the oval leaves are still a fresh green. In autumn, they slowly turn to red and gold, creating a brilliant splash of colour.

**PROPAGATION AND GROWING** Plant in late autumn or spring in light, lime-free soil into which peat or humus has previously been incorporated. Fothergillas tolerate light shade and usually need no pruning.

**VARIETIES** *F. major (above)*, rounded, bottle-brush-like spikes of cream flowers cover a spreading bush; *F. gardenii*, up to 90cm/3ft high but spreading to 1.2m/4ft, catkins of scented flowers appear on leafless branches in spring. *F. monticola*, very similar to *F. major* but if anything more vivid autumn colouring.

**POSSIBLE PROBLEMS** Generally trouble-free.

■ SPECIAL CARE TIP

*It is important to encourage bushiness while broom is young. Once the plant matures and becomes leggy, it cannot be cut back hard, as the old wood will not produce new shoots. A poor, free-draining soil gives the best results. Feeding will reduce the number of flowers produced.*

■ SPECIAL CARE TIP

*Although it tolerates shade quite happily, the rich autumn leaf colours of fothergilla develop best in full sun. Give some careful thought to the positioning of this acid-loving shrub so that it can be appreciated in both its main seasons of interest – spring and autumn.*

# PIERIS

spring

hardy

semi-shade

3m/10ft

5m/15ft

# COLQUHOUNIA

summer

half-hardy

full sun

3m/10ft

1.8m/6ft

Species of pieris are prized for their brilliant colouring rather than the slight fragrance of their waxy white blooms. The young leaves, narrow and pointed in shape, provide a fiery-red setting for large panicles of pure white flowers. As the season progresses the foliage turns green; all species are evergreen. As ericaceous plants, pieris hate lime. They are vulnerable to sharp winds and spring frosts, and must have a sheltered position. Plants take many years to reach the dimensions given, and can be successfully grown in containers – which is a good way of providing the correct growing medium if your garden's soil is inappropriate.

**PROPAGATION AND GROWING**  Plant in autumn or spring in moist, lime-free soil in a sheltered, lightly shaded position (pieris are shallow-rooting and may be scorched by hot sun). Keep moist at all times. Remove flowers as they fade. Propagate by cuttings taken in summer.

**VARIETIES**  *P. formosa forestii (above)*, *P. formosa* 'Forest Flame', elegant shape, young foliage pink and white, withstands frost well.

**POSSIBLE PROBLEMS**  Generally trouble-free.

Colquhounia (pronounced ka-hoon-e-a) owes its name to the plant collector who brought it to Europe from the Himalayas in the nineteenth-century. It belongs to the family *Labiatae*, along with lavender, rosemary, hyssop and thyme, and needs similar conditions to the Mediterranean herbs. Like its relatives, it has narrow, grey-green intensely aromatic leaves, but *C. coccinea (above)* steals the march on them in terms of flowers, bearing a mass of funnel-shaped scarlet and yellow blooms in late summer.

**PROPAGATION AND GROWING**  Plant in spring in light well-drained soil in full sun. This shrub needs the protection of a warm, sunny wall except in very mild districts, and should be covered in frosty weather. New plants are easy to raise from cuttings.

**VARIETIES**  *C. c. vestita*, a woolly-leaved type well-suited to drier conditions.

**POSSIBLE PROBLEMS**  Frost damage.

## ▇ SPECIAL CARE TIP

*If you have alkaline soil, it is not enough just to add peat or leaf mould to a border before planting. Lime will seep in from the surrounding soil and the* pieris *will sicken and probably die. A raised border or container is the solution, but use rainwater for watering.*

## ▇ PROPAGATION TIP

*Even in sheltered conditions,* colquhounia *can be cut back to the ground during cold winters, although it should recover in spring. As a precaution, propagate by taking cuttings during summer, then grow on in containers of free-draining compost, that can be moved into frost-free conditions.*

# AZALEAS

| spring | hardy | semi-shade | 90cm/3ft | 90cm/3ft |

The main difference between rhododendrons and azaleas is that most of the former are evergreen, most of the latter deciduous. The choice of scented types among the azaleas gives a very good choice of colour.

**PROPAGATION AND GROWING** Treat as rhododendrons. If growing azaleas in containers of ericaceous compost, take care to water with lime-free water, preferably rainwater.

**VARIETIES** *R. luteum*, 1.8m/6ft, heavily fragrant yellow flowers, the parent of many scented hybrids; *R. occidentale*, 3m/10ft, white, free-flowering; Ghent azaleas, especially 'Daviesii', cream blotched orange; 'Coccinea Rosa' *(above)*, 'Narcissiflora', double yellow, 'Corneille' cream and pink, 'Coccinea Speciosa' orange-red, 'Vulcan', deep red.

**POSSIBLE PROBLEMS** Azalea whitefly; azalea gall.

# ESCALLONIA

| summer | hardy | full sun | 3m/10ft | 1.8m/6ft |

Escallonias are one of the most rewarding evergreen shrubs, with glossy green leathery leaves and an abundance of pink, carmine or white flowers. The foliage is slightly sticky to the touch, sometimes with an aroma of balsam. Not all varieties are hardy in colder districts, where the protection of a warm, sunny wall is advisable. Quick-growing, they make good hedging plants and do well in seaside gardens.

**PROPAGATION AND GROWING** Set out young plants in autumn or spring on any good garden soil (escallonias are lime-tolerant). Remove flowering stems after the flowers have faded. For hedging, place 30cm/12in apart and cut back by one quarter after planting. Trim established hedges after flowering (but the harder they are pruned, the fewer the flowers).

**VARIETIES** *E. floribunda*, pure white fragrant flowers in long (up to 23cm/9in) panicles. *E. rubra* 'woodside' *(above)*, *E. pterocladon*, 7.5cm/3in long racemes of fragrant white flowers, one parent of a number of beautiful hybrids including the outstanding Donard strain from Northern Ireland: 'Donard Beauty', rose-red; 'Donard Gem', compact with pink flowers; 'Slieve Donard', pink flowers sometimes with a second showing in the autumn.

**POSSIBLE PROBLEMS** Silver leaf.

## SPECIAL CARE TIP

Azaleas *grown in containers of ericaceous compost or any acid, peaty soil benefit from being sprayed with rainwater during prolonged dry spells.*

## PLANTING TIP

Escallonias *make an excellent wind break, provided the temperature is not too low, and are quite happy growing in chalky, well-drained soil.*

# SAMBUCUS

| spring | hardy | semi-shade | 3.5m/12ft | 3.5m/12ft |

Perhaps because elders are so tolerant of severe conditions, their decorative value is overlooked in favour of their practical qualities. But decorative they are, with leaves divided into elegant leaflets, clusters of fragrant star-shaped flowers and an abundance of gleaming fruits.

**PROPAGATION AND GROWING** Container-grown plants can be set out at any time of year, on any type of soil. Water well if planted in late spring/summer. Prune specimens grown for their coloured foliage in winter, cutting back two-year-old wood to ground level and reducing one-year-old stems by half.

**VARIETIES** *S. racemosa* (Hart's elder), early flowering, panicle-like heads of white sweet-smelling blossom followed by scarlet fruits; foliage of the variety 'Plumosa Aurea' *(above)* is bright golden-green; *S. nigra* (common elder), up to 10m/30ft in the open, heads of musk-scented creamy flowers followed by masses of black berries (both blossom and fruit are used in wine-making); *S. n.* 'Aurea' (golden elder), brilliant yellow leaves. *S. canadensis* 'Maxima', huge heads of muscatel-scented flowers, blue-green foliage.

**POSSIBLE PROBLEMS** Aphids; arabis mosaic virus.

# GAULTHERIA

| summer | hardy | semi-shade | 15cm/6in | 90cm-1.2m/3-4ft |

Evergreen and spreading, *G. procumbens (above)* makes excellent ground cover and is very successful interplanted with species of Erica. Different as they appear – making a striking contrast of form and colour – gaultherias belong to the heather family and need very similar growing conditions. Small pale pink flowers are followed by bright scarlet fruits gleaming against the dark, glossy foliage.

**PROPAGATION AND GROWING** Plant between autumn and spring in moist well-drained acid soil. Mulch from time to time with peat or leaf mould. Thin overcrowded shoots after flowering if necessary.

**VARIETIES** *G. procumbens* (wintergreen, checkerberry), aromatic rather than fragrant, waxy flowers like lily-of-the-valley on red stems. One of the best ground-cover plants. *G. fragrantissima*, up to 1.4m/4ft 6in in height, racemes of fragrant pale pink flowers on scarlet stems. The fragrance is easily appreciated if flowers are cut and used in indoor arrangements. Dark blue berries in the autumn.

**POSSIBLE PROBLEMS** Generally trouble-free.

## ▨ PLANTING TIP

*For those who would like to grow acers but have the wrong conditions, this plant is a superb substitute for some of the golden-leaved kinds.*

## ▨ ORGANIC TIP

*The thick ground cover provided by gaultheria is the best defence against weeds, which would otherwise have to be sprayed or dug up.*

# SKIMMIA

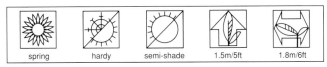

| spring | hardy | semi-shade | 1.5m/5ft | 1.8m/6ft |

When crushed, the beautiful leaves of *S. japonica* exude the scent of oranges. This fine shrub has many other qualities besides: a slow-growing evergreen with pale green oval leaves, it bears panicles of fragrant, creamy flowers in early spring. These are followed (on female plants) by round bright red berries which remain on the plant throughout the winter. Skimmias do well in town and seaside gardens.

**PROPAGATION AND GROWING** Plant in autumn or spring in any type of well-drained soil, in sun or partial shade. In an exposed position, frost may damage the young foliage. No pruning is necessary. Propagate from cuttings of side-shoots taken in summer. To produce berries, both female and male plants must be grown together.

**VARIETIES** *S. japonica*, female; 'Fragrans' is a male form with an intense fragrance; *S.* × 'Foremanii', female *(above)*, dark green leaves; *S. reevesiana*, female, compact in size and shape, pointed mid-green leaves, oval berries; *S. r.* 'Rubella' is a male form. Both dislike lime.

**POSSIBLE PROBLEMS** None in suitable conditions.

# LUPINUS

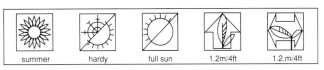

| summer | hardy | full sun | 1.2m/4ft | 1.2.m/4ft |

Perennial lupins are a familiar sight in herbaceous borders, with tall colourful spikes of flowers. Less widely cultivated is their shrubby cousin the tree lupin, *L. arboreus (above)*, with 15cm/6in racemes of flowers which are usually yellow, but sometimes lilac or blue. This fast-growing shrub is a useful plant for informal gardens and for making a speedy effect in new plantings. It does well in seaside gardens. Although it is short-lived, the tree lupin self-seeds readily.

**PROPAGATION AND GROWING** Plant between autumn and spring on well-drained soil, in a sunny position. Prune to shape after flowering. New plants come true from seed.

**VARIETIES** There are no named varieties.

**POSSIBLE PROBLEMS** Generally trouble-free.

## SPECIAL CARE TIP

*Too much sun can cause yellowing of the leaves in* skimmias, *but this can also be a sign of alkaline soil. Check soil pH to be sure.*

## PROPAGATION TIP

*The tree lupin will reach flowering size in the second year after sowing, and by the third year will have grown to its full height and spread.*

111

# CISTUS

| summer | hardy | full sun | 1.8m/6ft | 90cm/3ft |

The rock roses or sun roses, as cistus are called, are evergreen Mediterranean plants with aromatic leaves. The scent is stronger in the noon-day heat, reminiscent of sun-baked hillsides in the south of France. Papery flowers of white, red or pink appear in profusion for several weeks in early summer.

**PROPAGATION AND GROWING**  Plant in late spring on well-drained, even poor soil, in full sun. Cistus do well on chalky soil. Protect from winds. Prune in spring to remove stems damaged by frost. Propagate from seed or cuttings taken in late summer.

**VARIETIES**  *C. laurifolius*, dull green pointed-oval leaves, with clusters of 5cm/2in wide white flowers, the hardiest species; *C. × purpureus (above)* up to 1.2m/4ft, handsome 7.5cm/3in wide red-purple flowers, may not survive a severe winter.

**POSSIBLE PROBLEMS**  Frost damage.

# PAEONIA

| summer | hardy | full sun | 1.8m/6ft | 1.8m/6ft |

Buttercups and peonies are the David and Goliath of the ranunculus family, though it is only in respect of their relative size that shrubby peonies resemble the Biblical character. Most are Chinese in origin, very beautiful, very hardy garden plants with cup-shaped, sometimes double flowers up to 15cm/6in across, more in some species. They form dense clumps of handsome foliage, wonderful in borders or as specimens in a lawn. Two of the species include fragrant varieties.

**PROPAGATION AND GROWING**  Peonies are lime-tolerant, and like moist, well-drained soil into which well-rotted compost has been incorporated. Plant between autumn and spring, taking care to bury the union of stock and scion. Position out of early morning sun, which may cause damage after night frost. Water well. Remove flowers as they fade. Cut out dead wood in spring. Propagate by carefully removing rooted suckers or by layering.

**VARIETIES**  *P. suffruticosa fragrans maxima-plena*, very large salmon pink double flowers; 'Elizabeth' *(above)*; 'Mrs George Warre', vigorous hybrid, deep pink flowers; *P. lutea*, pale green leaves, 5cm/2in single yellow flowers, scent of lilies; 'Souvenir de Maxime Cornu', hybrid, 1.3m/4ft 6 in high, buttercup yellow double flowers edged deep pink.

**POSSIBLE PROBLEMS**  Honey fungus; peony wilt.

## ▪ PLANTING TIP

Cistus *combine very well with other Mediterranean plants, such as lavender and rosemary. Since they all thrive in roughly the same conditions, they would be* ideal for a sun-drenched border, perhaps near a gravel path or stone terrace where the reflected heat will bring out the scent of the leaves.

## ▪ PLANTING TIP

Tree peonies, despite their common name, are bushy plants well-suited to a sheltered mixed border. Their blooms are so large and exotic, however, that they should really be planted so that they can be enjoyed without distraction from other plants during flowering, in late spring and early summer.

# CLERODENDRUM

| summer | half-hardy | full sun | 1.8m/6ft | 1.8m/6ft |

Few clerodendrums are hardy enough to grow outdoors; two, both natives of the Far East, bear fragrant flowers. The foliage, however, emits an unpleasant smell if crushed. These are showy, interesting plants of the verbena family, candidates for a favoured position.

**PROPAGATION AND GROWING** Plant in autumn or spring on fertile, well-drained soil in a sunny, sheltered spot. Prune in spring, if necessary, to remove frost-damaged shoots.

**VARIETIES** *C. bungei (above)*, deciduous, heart-shaped leaves, broad heads of rose-pink flowers on tall slender stems; *C. trichomotum*, deciduous, oval leaves, large clusters of star-shaped pale pink flowers followed by kingfisher blue berries.

**POSSIBLE PROBLEMS** None in suitable conditions.

# NYMPHAEA

| summer | hardy | full sun | 15-20cm/6-8in | 2.5m/8ft |

Do not imagine that their exotic appearance means that waterlilies are only for stately gardens. While many species are too large for the average garden pool, some will do very well in small pools, and several are sweetly scented. Long strong roots go down into the mud, anchoring the rootstock from which leaves and flower-stems arise. It is important to give plants the correct depth of water, but the hardy species need very little attention once established.

**PROPAGATION AND GROWING** Plant in spring in clear water. Set directly into fertile soil; sometimes nymphaea are sold in containers for planting which will eventually rot when the plant is established. Propagate by offsets taken in spring.

**VARIETIES** *N. odorata* 'Turicensis', depth 30cm/12in, spread 75cm/2ft 6in, pale pink flowers; *N. tuberosa rosea* (magnolia water lily), depth 90cm/3ft, spread 1.2m/4ft and extending over time, very fragrant pink flowers; 'James Brydon' *(above)*.

**POSSIBLE PROBLEMS** Aphids; beetles; leaf spot.

## SPECIAL CARE TIP

*In ideal conditions,* clerodendrum *can grow to be larger than expected, but it can easily be kept in check by hard pruning in mid-spring.*

## ORGANIC TIP

*Even small gardens can include a water feature. With a good balance of plants, frogs may take up residence, and then your slug problems will be over.*

## RIBES

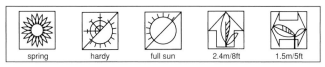

| spring | hardy | full sun | 2.4m/8ft | 1.5m/5ft |

Ornamental currants make large, showy shrubs with a fruity scent, suitable for informal gardens. The species *R. sanguineum* (flowering currant) is widely grown but perhaps not always wisely planted. Covered with rich, rose-red flowers, it looks best set in a closely planted mixed border, perhaps with deep pink tulips, mounds of cranesbills and the dense foliage of alchemilla. All species bear fruits, which are not edible.

**PROPAGATION AND GROWING** Plant from autumn to spring in any type of well-drained soil in sun or partial shade. Thin weak and damaged wood after flowering. Propagate by hardwood cuttings taken in late autumn.

**VARIETIES** *R. sanguineum* 'Pulborough Scarlet' *(above)*; *R. s.*'Splendens', long sprays of pink flowers, foliage aromatic when bruised; 'King Edward VII', racemes of deep crimson flowers, aromatic leaves, blue-black fruits. *R. aureum* syn. *R. odoratum*, clove-scented yellow flowers, black fruits against golden foliage in autumn.

**POSSIBLE PROBLEMS** Aphids; leaf spot.

## ERICA

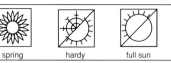

| spring | hardy | full sun | 60cm/2ft | 90cm/3ft |

Of the enormous number of heaths and heathers, only a few are fragrant. *E. arborea* is one, but few gardens can fit it in, at a possible mature height of 6m/20ft. *E. mediterranea* is another, only half that height but not reliably hardy. The most reliable choice is the hybrid *E. × darleyensis (above)*, a vigorous grower that begins to make an appearance in the middle of winter. It looks best closely interplanted with other heathers, possibly other varieties of the same species.

**PROPAGATION AND GROWING** Grow in groups of five or six set 30cm/12in apart. Plant in autumn or late spring in full sun, in soil that has previously been well dug over. Unlike many heaths, *E. × darleyensis* will grow well on chalky soil. Keep moist after planting – water well, particularly during the first year. Mulch with peat to retain moisture. Cut the plants back after flowering.

**VARIETIES** *E. × darleyensis* 'Silberschmelze' (also known as 'Molten Silver'), white flowers; *E. ×* 'George Rendall', pale green leaf, pink flowers.

**POSSIBLE PROBLEMS** Generally trouble-free.

■ PLANTING TIP

*More unusual are the white-flowered forms, 'Albescens' which is a pinkish-white, and 'Tydeman's White' which is pure white.*

■ PLANTING TIP

*In areas of alkaline soil, extend the period of interest with heathers by planting varieties of the earlier flowering Erica carnea.*

## LIPPIA

|  |  |  |  |  |
|---|---|---|---|---|
| summer | half hardy | full sun | 1.5m/5ft | 1.2m/4ft |

Lemon-scented verbena, *L. citriodora* syn. *Aloysia triphylla (above)*, is a native of Chile, which in cooler climates needs the protection of a warm, sunny wall. It makes a rather sprawling bush, which in late summer bears panicles of lavender flowers. The delicious scent is in the long, narrow leaves and is released at the lightest touch, especially on hot days.

**PROPAGATION AND GROWING** Plant in early summer in any type of well-drained soil – lippia withstands drought well – in a sunny, sheltered position. Prune established shrubs in spring, taking the main branches back to 30cm/12in. Cut side shoots to 2-3 buds from the old wood. Propagate from cuttings taken in summer.

**VARIETIES** There are no named varieties.

**POSSIBLE PROBLEMS** Generally trouble-free.

## CEANOTHUS

|  |  |  |  |  |
|---|---|---|---|---|
| summer | hardy | full sun | 3m/10ft | 2.1m/7ft |

Ceanothus, commonly known as Californian lilacs, are among the most beautiful flowering shrubs. Like carpenterias *(see page 95)*, they need a warm sheltered spot to thrive. The fragrance is in the breathtaking blue flowers of two hybrids.

**PROPAGATION AND GROWING** Set out container-grown plants in late spring against a warm, sunny wall, in light well-drained soil. To ensure maximum exposure to light, evegreens should have their shoots and branches attached to supports. Remove flowers as they fade. Prune lightly after flowering to keep the shape neat. Propagate from cuttings taken in summer.

**VARIETIES** C. × 'Burkwoodii', evergreen, with a wide, spreading habit, 5cm/2in long panicles of bright blue flowers; C. × 'Gloire de Versailles' *(above)*, deciduous, large leaves, 20cm/8in panicles of powder blue flowers. May be hard-pruned to shape for formal plantings.

**POSSIBLE PROBLEMS** Scale insects; honey fungus; frost damage.

### ■ SPECIAL CARE TIP

*As the scented leaves of* lippia *appear relatively late, and are frost tender, a sheltered, sunny spot is essential to let this shrub perform at its best.*

### ■ PLANTING TIP

*The particular soft shade of blue of 'Gloire de Versailles' makes it ideal for the mixed border where it blends well with perennials.*

# TREES AND CLIMBERS

**Well trained and maintained trees and climbers can give your garden an established, timeless look. In a new garden, often open to the elements on three sides, planting some suitable trees and running climbers up walls and fences soon takes away that brand new feel.**

Even tiny gardens can benefit from the unique effects that a tree can give - dappled shade, a green canopy, bird song through upstairs windows, and the sound of rustling leaves. Add to these a tree with scented flowers or leaves, and you have an irresistible asset for the garden. For large gardens, the choice is wider, and imposing effects can be created with variations of perspective, shade, colour, shape and fragrance.

From the point of view of your garden's health, a tree is an excellent addition. Providing a home for birds and beneficial insects, it will help you establish a balanced ecosystem in your garden that will allow you to avoid using chemical pesticides altogether. In an exposed garden, it can also help provide that elusive quality — shelter — which is so important in growing tender plants and in helping to keep the scent of aromatics right where you want it.

**LONG-TERM PLANNING**  Planting a tree should not be undertaken lightly. It is a feature that is likely to stay with you for as long as you stay with the garden. Whether you choose a little robinia as a specimen tree in your town garden or a huge lime or even an avenue of limes for your country estate, think about the effect of the tree on the surroundings and of the surroundings on the tree. Look at aspect, light and shade, exposure and shelter, and mean temperatures. Think about the outline of the tree, not only in summer but in all seasons. Will it enhance the other planting? Will the leaf colour tone in? Will it still be an asset in 10 or 20 years time? Only when you have satisfied yourself on these points should you go ahead and plant your tree.

**PLANTING FOR POSTERITY**  Give your tree the best possible chance of growing to maturity by planting it with care. Bare-rooted trees should be planted at the same depth as they were in the nursery. The correct depth is easy to see with pot-grown specimens. Dig a hole sufficiently deep and wide to accommodate the bare roots when spread out or large enough to take the container and leave room for thorough back filling with soil enriched with well-rotted organic matter and bone meal. Fork over the base of the planting hole to ensure good drainage, then place a layer of the enriched soil in the base. Sit the tree on top and make any adjustments for depth. Fill around the plant, firming gently with the foot, to ensure that no air pockets have been left around the roots. Finally, water in the tree thoroughly. Continue to water regularly during the first year, at least.

If you are staking a bare-rooted tree, drive the stake down into the bottom of the planting hole before planting. Place it on the side from which the prevailing wind blows, and fasten the tree to it with adjustable ties. For container grown trees, stake after planting, with a stake driven obliquely into the ground to the side towards which the prevailing wind blows. Again, use adjustable ties. They should be checked regularly as the tree grows.

**CLIMBERS** By training climbers upwards against a wall, over a purpose built structure or through trees or other shrubs, you create vertical interest and, most importantly, bring scent up to a level at which it can be best appreciated. Climbing shrubs trained around a door make a spectacular entrance and allow scent to enter the house each time the door opens. Jasmine and honeysuckle are favourites for such a position, but the choice is extensive. Training climbers, particularly close to the house, is very important as they can look untidy and reduce light if left to themselves and, in many cases, will not flower so well. By providing a firm framework of wires or trellis from the outset and guiding new shoots to cover it, most climbers can be kept manageable without excessive pruning. Some will cling to supports themselves while others need to be tied in, but they are all worth looking after and will repay your care.

**CLIMBING COMBINATIONS** Combining climbers with trees or shrubs and allowing them to scramble up and through established woody plants produces an informal effect that should be reflected in your choice of plants. An old apple tree with a clematis twining through its branches, for example, is an excellent combination. Firstly, a large apple tree is strong enough to support even the most vigourous of clematis without suffering itself. Secondly, the season of interest is greatly extended by choosing summer flowering clematis to follow on from the apple blossom. Thirdly, the loose, open growth of the clematis matches the relaxed and traditional look of the tree. Even without the advantages of scent, it is successful planting, but by choosing a scented clematis, an even more memorable effect is produced. Another possible combination is to plant an early-flowering clematis with a later-flowering shrub, such as philadelphus. With careful selection, you can combine climbers with shrubs and trees to double the length of the season of interest or to intensify it with simultaneous flowering.

**GARDEN STRUCTURES** Climbers add another dimension to sitting-out areas, and the addition of scent creates a special, romantic atmosphere in bowers or pergolas. Choose specimens that are particularly well-scented at night, for areas where you sit outside on warm evenings. The training of climbers in such a situation need not be quite so formal. The main objective is to cover the structure with the climber, so regular tying in to form a framework of shoots during the early years after planting is all that is required. An important point to remember when using wooden structures for climbers is that certain chemicals commonly used for treating wood give off fumes that will kill plants. If you are using any form of wood preservative on a structure that you intend to use near plants, check the label to make sure that it is safe for that purpose, then relax and enjoy the unique atmosphere that scented climbers create.

**PLANTING CLIMBERS** Like trees, climbers are likely to stay in position for many years, so many of the same planting considerations apply. Make sure that the aspect is suitable for the climber of your choice. There are types suitable to almost any position, so do not let a sentimental attachment to wisteria blind you to the fact that the front of your house is in shade for most of the day. Instead of making an expensive mistake, work with nature and plant a clematis or honeysuckle, and build a pergola for your wisteria.

Apply the same rules for clearing perennial weeds, improving the soil by adding well-rotted organic matter, and digging a planting hole larger than the root ball of your plant. Many climbers are rapid growers and produce a great deal of lush growth every year, so include some bone meal in the planting hole to help with root development, and feed yearly in spring.

Climbers planted close to a solid object, whether walls or trees, often have problems with a water shortage, particularly if there are overhanging eaves or branches. Plant at least 45 cm/18 in away from the support, with the roots pointing out towards open ground, and guide the climbing shoots in towards it. Water generously at all times of year.

## Fraxinus

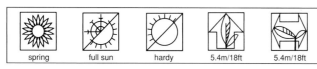

| spring | full sun | hardy | 5.4m/18ft | 5.4m/18ft |

There are many species of ash, some too large for the average garden, but all are shapely trees with characteristically pinnate leaves. There are two species of a size manageable in average gardens, both with scented blooms flowering in spring.

**PROPAGATION AND GROWING** Ashes are hardy, even in exposed positions, and do well in towns or seaside locations. They grow best in deep loam. Plant from autumn to spring in sun or semi-shade. Keep reasonably moist at all times. No pruning is necessary.

**VARIETIES** *F. ornus (above)*, the manna ash, an elegant tree with deep olive-green foliage. Dense panicles of heavily fragrant white flowers with a scent of honey in late spring. *F. mariesii*, grey, downy buds precede tiny cream flowers in scented clusters, late spring, followed by small purple fruits in summer.

**POSSIBLE PROBLEMS** Ash canker; honey fungus.

## Robinia

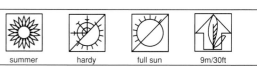

| summer | hardy | full sun | 9m/30ft | 4.5m/15ft |

The group of trees known as false acacias is related to both laburnum and wisteria, as is obvious from the racemes of pea-shaped flowers which they all bear. Of the three species in cultivation, only one bears fragrant flowers. *R. pseudoacacia (above)*, native to the United States, is a deciduous tree with graceful, light green foliage and deep grooves in the bark of the stem. Racemes of scented, creamy-coloured flowers, up to 18cm/7in long, appear in early summer. Often grown as standard specimens, robinias do well in town gardens or can be grown as wall shrubs.

**PROPAGATION AND GROWING** Plant between autumn and spring in any ordinary, well-drained soil in a situation where the tree will be given some protection from strong winds. Pruning is not necessary.

**VARIETIES** *R.* 'Frisia', new leaves of golden-yellow turn light, very sharp green in summer – an arresting sight.

**POSSIBLE PROBLEMS** Generally trouble-free.

### ▨ PLANTING TIP

*Although suitable for gardens, the above species must be planted far enough from the house to prevent the roots causing damage to drains or foundations.*

### ▨ PLANTING TIP

*The best flowering is achieved when robinia is planted in full sun, but shelter from wind is even more important, as the branches are brittle. This* *makes it unsuitable for coastal areas, but it is perfect for small town gardens, where its tolerance of pollution is a most important feature.*

# LABURNUM

| summer | hardy | full sun | 7.5m/25ft | 4.5m.15ft |

Laburnums are familiarly known as golden rain trees because of the effect produced by countless racemes of bright yellow flowers in spring or early summer. They make spectacular specimen trees and in at least one famous garden have been planted in a double row to form a floriferous avenue. The pea-shaped, lightly fragrant flowers are followed by dull parchment-coloured seed pods, which are extremely poisonous.

**PROPAGATION AND GROWING** Plant between autumn and spring in any type of well-drained soil. Laburnums prefer sun, but will tolerate light shade. Provide stakes to support the newly planted tree. No pruning is necessary.

**VARIETIES** *L. alpinum* or Scotch laburnum *(above)*, spreading habit, handsome bark in maturity, flowers in 25cm/10in racemes; 'Pyramidalis' is an erect form; *L. anagyroides* (common laburnum), 3m/10ft high, sometimes more, an early-flowering species with racemes 15-25cm/6-10in long. Named varieties include 'Pendulum', with a weeping habit, good for small gardens. *L. × watereri*, hybrid of moderate height. The variety 'Vossii' bears abundant racemes up to 50cm/20in long.

**POSSIBLE PROBLEMS** Honey fungus; leaf miners.

# AESCULUS

| summer | hardy | sun | 12m/40ft | 10m/30ft |

The horse chestnut is probably one of the showiest of big trees, the grand specimens gracing parks and the gardens of stately country houses. The most fragrant species, *A. californica (above)*, eventually reaches 12m/40ft, which excludes it from small gardens. It bears the chestnut's characteristic 'candles' (panicles of tiny flowers) up to 20cm/8in long, white flushed rose and with a sweet scent. The rough fruits that follow are pear-shaped.

**PROPAGATION AND GROWING** Aesculus species like a deep, loamy, well-drained soil. Plant between autumn and spring in a sunny or partially shaded position. Pruning is not necessary.

**VARIETIES** There are no named varieties.

**POSSIBLE PROBLEMS** Leaf spot.

## SPECIAL CARE TIP

*An advantage of the highly decorative 'Vossii', is that it is partly sterile and so produces fewer of the poisonous seeds than the other types.*

## SPECIAL CARE TIP

*Look out for damaged or dead wood on horse chestnuts, and cut it out as soon as possible, or it may become infected with coral-spot fungus.*

## EUCRYPHIA

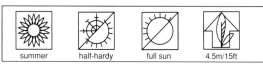

| | | | | |
|---|---|---|---|---|
| summer | half-hardy | full sun | 4.5m/15ft | 2.4m/8ft |

Eucryphias are ornamental trees which are only hardy in favoured districts. If you can provide the warmth and shelter they need, you will be rewarded with a display of exquisite, scented flowers in late summer. Cream or white, the cup-shaped blooms are at least 5cm/2in across with prominent stamens, rather like a single rose in form. Some species are evergreen.

**PROPAGATION AND GROWING** Plant the species described in autumn (less hardy species must wait until late spring) on light, acid soil. Like clematis, eucryphias need a cool root run, so will not thrive in the open exposed to full sun. A sheltered position is best. Newly planted trees need protection from frost in the winter. Pruning is not necessary, but it is advisable to pinch out the leading shoots of young plants. Propagate by cuttings taken in summer.

**VARIETIES** *E. × nymansensis*, evergreen hybrid, upright habit, quick-growing, flowers singly or in clusters. 'Nymansay' *(above)* is a beautiful variety. *E. glutinosa* to 3m/10ft, lime tolerant evergreen, slow-growing. This is the hardiest type with spectacular flowers; the foliage turns red in autumn.

**POSSIBLE PROBLEMS** Generally trouble-free.

## STUARTIA

| | | | | |
|---|---|---|---|---|
| summer | hardy | semi-shade | 6m/20ft | 4.5m/15ft |

The stuartias (or stewartias, as they are sometimes listed), are happiest in a damp woodland garden and are fairly hardy in mild districts. All are deciduous and bear beautiful cup-shaped flowers, which in only one species are fragrant. This is *S. sinensis (above)*, from China, with oval bright green leaves and 5cm/2in wide white flowers with showy stamens. The bark peels away, leaving the stem smooth and grey. In autumn the foliage turns a gorgeous shade of red.

**PROPAGATION AND GROWING** Plant in spring in well-drained soil to which plenty of peat has been added – stuartias like an acid soil. No pruning or special care is needed, indeed any disturbance is resented.

**VARIETIES** There are no named varieties.

**POSSIBLE PROBLEMS** Generally trouble-free.

---

### ■ SPECIAL CARE TIP

*Although spectacular once mature enough to flower, 'Nymansay' takes several years to reach flowering size and, as it greatly resents root disturbance, it must be planted as a small, pot-grown specimen. It grows quickly if protected from frost, but the roots are very shallow and easily damaged.*

### ■ PLANTING TIP

*The best results are obtained from stuartia when the roots are given some shade, but the shoots are in the sun with shelter from strong winds.*

# CRATAEGUS

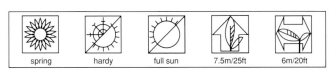

| spring | hardy | full sun | 7.5m/25ft | 6m/20ft |

Hawthorns are members of the rose family, as their sharp thorns indicate. The botanical name *Crataegus* comes from a Greek word meaning strength, a reference to the hardness of the wood which accurately describes the tough character of these ornamental trees. They tolerate drought and pollution, do well in seaside gardens and in exposed positions. Heavy with blossom in spring and bright with berries (haws) in autumn, they deserve to be more widely planted. One species can be used for hedging.

**PROPAGATION AND GROWING**  Plant in winter in any type of soil. No pruning is necessary. For hedges, set young plants 37cm/15in apart. When established trim in summer.

**VARIETIES**  *C. monogyna*, common hawthorn *(above)*, thorny, heavily scented, white flowers, clusters of small deep red haws, glossy leaves, good for hedging; the variety 'biflora' bears a second flush of flowers in mild winters. *C. × lavallei* syn. *C. carrierei*, has few thorns, glossy leaves, cream flowers, long-lasting orange haws; also varieties of *C. oxycantha* syn. *C. laevigata* make good specimen trees, especially 'Coccinea Plena', double scarlet flowers, 'Alba Plena', double white turning pink, 'Candida Plena', double pure white.

**POSSIBLE PROBLEMS**  Caterpillars; leaf spot.

# HALESIA

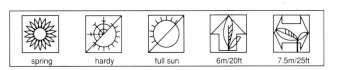

| spring | hardy | full sun | 6m/20ft | 7.5m/25ft |

Pendulous white flowers earn halesias the common name of snowdrop tree or silver bell tree. Native to North America, there are two species bearing scented blossom in late spring. Curious four-winged fruits succeed the flowers. The light green leaves are oval in shape. As the habit of growth is somewhat spreading, neither is suitable for small gardens.

**PROPAGATION AND GROWING**  Halesias hate lime. Plant in autumn or spring in moist, acid, peaty soil in sun or dappled shade. These preferences make halesias ideal woodland plants. No pruning is necessary.

**VARIETIES**  *H. carolina (above)*, clusters of 1cm/½in long flowers; *H. monticola* with slightly large flowers, is the more fragrant type. The variety *H. m.* 'Rosea' bears pale pink flowers.

**POSSIBLE PROBLEMS**  Generally trouble-free.

---

■ SPECIAL CARE TIP

*Hawthorn is a popular hedging plant for farms, as it grows quickly to form a strong, prickly barrier. Grown on its own, however, it soon goes bare at the base. Try combining it with other, denser hedging plants, such as beech, holly or hornbeam, to provide a decorative habitat for wildlife.*

■ PLANTING TIP

*This large tree casts only dappled shade, and is therefore suitable for underplanting with acid-loving plants, such as camellias and rhododendrons.*

## EUCALYPTUS

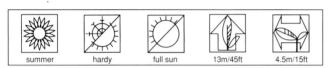

| summer | hardy | full sun | 13m/45ft | 4.5m/15ft |

The cider gum, *E. gunnii (above)*, is a fast-growing evergreen which will reach the dimensions given in 10 years. Frequent cutting back, however, will keep the size within bounds and encourage the maintenance of the attractive juvenile leaves which are one of the tree's main attractions. The foliage of almost all species of eucalyptus changes in the second or third year to an adult form which is very different from the immature tree's leaves. (*E. cordata* is an exception.) *E. gunnii* has bluish-green, almost perfectly round leaves which change to a narrow, pointed shape in the second or third year. If it is planted against a wall – protection which it will appreciate – the fluttering leaves cast a delicate shadow in brilliant sunshine. White, scented flowers appear in clusters during the summer. The creamy bark peels away to reveal dove-grey colouring beneath. These qualities make the eucalyptus an outstanding specimen tree.

**PROPAGATION AND GROWING** This is the hardiest of the eucalyptus, but still vulnerable to damage by wind. Place in a sheltered position and stake firmly when young. Plant in spring in well-drained soil and keep well watered in dry spells.

**VARIETIES** There are no varieties of the species, which is sometimes known as *E. whittingehamensis.*

**POSSIBLE PROBLEMS** Sucking insects on juvenile foliage.

## TILIA

| summer | hardy | full sun | 7.5m/25ft | 4.5m/15ft |

Lime or linden trees are a familiar sight in parks and public gardens; they are fast-growing deciduous trees and make handsome specimens. Unfortunately some are prone to infestation by aphids, which exude a rather sticky substance. One, *T petiolaris (above)*, the pendant silver lime, bears sweetly fragrant flowers which decorate the drooping, slender branches in summer. The leaves are rounded, as in most limes, but covered in fine down on top and white-felted underneath. The overall effect is silvery and very graceful.

**PROPAGATION AND GROWING** Plant from autumn to spring in any type of moist, but well-drained soil in full sun or semi-shade. Limes are often pollarded to shape when grown in public places or as stately avenues, but no regular pruning is necessary. Remove any suckers that arise from the main stem.

**VARIETIES** There are no named varieties.

**POSSIBLE PROBLEMS** Caterpillars; gall mites; die back.

### ▥ PLANTING TIP

Eucalyptus *are best planted very young, as pot-grown seedlings, preferably no taller than 30cm/1ft . These will establish well, and as they are such fast-growing* trees, *this should be no hardship. The juvenile leaves are popular with flower arrangers and can be glycerined to preserve them.*

### ▥ ORGANIC TIP

Limes are very attractive to bees, as well as less beneficial insects, but T. petiolaris, *is resistant to aphid, which can be a troublesome pest.*

## JASMINUM

| summer | hardy | full sun | 9m/30ft | climber |

Plants like jasmine, which have every appearance of fragility but are in fact vigorous and hardy, are a blessing to gardeners. The flowers of the common jasmine are pure white, *Jasminum officinale (above)*, numerous and very sweetly scented. First appearing in early summer, they persist for up to five months. This deciduous plant is a self-supporting climber with a twining habit of growth. Native to Persia, it has been popular in European gardens for half a century.

**PROPAGATION AND GROWING** Plant in spring on any type of well-drained soil against a sunny wall. Prune in spring, simply removing old and weak growth. Propagate by cuttings taken in summer.

**VARIETIES** *J. o. aureum*, leaves splashed gold; *J. o. affine*, larger flowers than the species.

**POSSIBLE PROBLEMS** Aphids.

## TRACHELOSPERMUM

| summer | hardy | full sun | up to 6m/20ft | climber |

Trachelospermums are oriental evergreen shrubs suitable for covering walls and fences. Dark green, shiny pointed leaves provide a dramatic background for the 7.5cm/3in wide white five-petalled flowers with yellow stamens.

**PROPAGATION AND GROWING** Plant in late spring, setting the plants in well-drained acid soil against a sunny wall. Trachelospermums are self-clinging and twining but need the support of light sticks when young. Remove flowerheads when they have faded. Thin out overcrowded shoots in spring if necessary. Propagate by layering.

**VARIETIES** *T. majus* syn. *T. japonicum*, very vigorous, reliably hardy, foliage bronzed and red in autumn, slightly fragrant flowers – this species will cover a house like ivy. *T. jasminoides (above)*, up to 4m/12ft, very fragrant flowers, a variegated form is available; *T. asiaticum*, very leafy, with yellowish white flowers.

**POSSIBLE PROBLEMS** Aphids.

### ▨ PLANTING TIP

*When siting jasmine in the fragrant garden, remember that its perfume is richest in the evening and night. It can make an outdoor dining area unforgettable.*

### ▨ PLANTING TIP

*Climbers suffer from lack of water if planted too close to a wall. They should be planted no less than 45cm/18in away from the wall, and more if there are overhanging eaves. Evergreens, such as trachelospermum need water all year round, so don't neglect them, particularly in a dry winter.*

# LONICERA

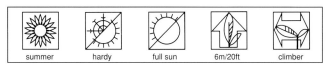

| summer | hardy | full sun | 6m/20ft | climber |

Honeysuckles (*Lonicera spp*) are one of the first plants that come to mind when planning a scented garden. Most of them are deliciously fragrant and endearingly easy to grow, with attractive foliage setting off the unusual flowers. The tangling mass of stems, heavy with scented blossom, is an essential feature of old-fashioned gardens.

**PROPAGATION AND GROWING** Plant between autumn and spring, in well-cultivated moisture-retentive soil. Honeysuckles (and clematis, which make good companions) like their heads in sun, their roots in cooler shade – which can be achieved by planting low-growing perennials at the base. Cut back long shoots after flowering to maintain a neat shape.

**VARIETIES** *L. periclymenum*, woodbine *(above)*, creamy-yellow flowers flushed pink in late summer, followed by scarlet berries. Two widely grown varieties are 'Belgica' (early Dutch honeysuckle), pink and yellow flowers in early summer and 'Serotina' (late Dutch honeysuckle), deep pink flowers white within, from mid-summer to autumn. *L. japonica*, evergreen, a compact species which bears small white flowers all summer.

**POSSIBLE PROBLEMS** Aphids; leaf spot.

# CLEMATIS

| summer | hardy | full sun | 6m/20ft | climber |

Clematis are justifiably one of the most popular climbers. Their scrambling, twining habit of growth suits the cottage-garden style and the choice of species and hybrids offers something for every situation. Foliage is as varied as flower size and colour, but among the species which provide scent, delicacy is the keynote.

**PROPAGATION AND GROWING** Plant between autumn and spring in alkaline soil, or add a little lime to the planting hole. The ideal position is one where the lower stem and roots can be shaded from the sun. Keep well watered. Prune hard and mulch annually in spring.

**VARIETIES** *C. viticella*, fast-growing with saucer-shaped purple flowers; *C. v. rubra*, highly recommended variety with deep crimson flowers; *C. v.* 'Minuet', cream-coloured flowers edged mauve. *C. montana* 'Elizabeth' *(above)*; *C. montana* 'Wilsonii', creamy-white with yellow stamens, strong scent; *C.armandii*, evergreen, waxy-white flowers; *C. heracleifolia* 'Wyevale', herbaceous species, huge hyacinth blue flowers.

**POSSIBLE PROBLEMS** Clematis wilt; earwigs.

## ▦ PLANTING TIP

*Honeysuckle is a vigorous climber and can swamp more delicate plants. If you are growing it through a shrub, make sure the two plants are equally matched.*

## ▦ SPECIAL CARE TIP

*Clematis wilt can act with distressing speed, causing seemingly healthy specimens to die back to ground level. Luckily, the fungus does not extend into* *the ground, so by planting clematis deeply, with at least one pair of leaves below the ground, there will be healthy shoots to grow up again.*

TREES AND CLIMBERS

# PASSIFLORA

| summer | half-hardy | full sun | 9m/30ft | 6m/20ft |

*Passiflora caerulea (above)* is a native of Brazil, a climber which can be grown on a sheltered wall in most districts. In mild localities it is evergreen. Exotic, star-shaped flowers with prominent stamens appear throughout the summer, and are sometimes followed by oval orange-red fruits. The flowers may be up to 18cm/7in across and are lightly fragrant. The plant acquired its common name – passion flower – from South American missionaries who saw in the form of the flowers a connection with the crucifixion of Christ; the crown of thorns, perhaps.

**PROPAGATION AND GROWING** Plant in late spring in well-drained soil in a sheltered position against a warm sunny wall with trellis or wires for support. Tie in the young growths. Protect over winter; plants may be cut down by frost, but new shoots will arise from the base. Prune in spring to remove frost-damaged stems.

**VARIETIES** *P. c.* 'Constance Elliott', pure white flowers.

**POSSIBLE PROBLEMS** Cucumber mosaic virus.

# WISTERIA

| spring | hardy | full sun | 30m/100ft | 18m/60ft |

Wisterias belong to the pea family, which makes them cousins to laburnums, brooms and the sweet pea, all fragrant and with the characteristic pea blossom. Perhaps they are grandfathers rather than cousins, since wisterias reach such a stupendous size and have an air of antique charm, with their pale if abundant flowers and their gnarled, twisted stems. The twining habit needs the support of wires if grown against a wall. Alternatively, wisterias can be trained over an archway or left to clothe an old tree. All varieties are fragrant.

**PROPAGATION AND GROWING** Plant in autumn or spring on any type of fertile soil, in a site where the roots will have plenty of room to spread. Wisterias are often seen against a warm sunny wall of a house, and this suits them very well. In winter, prune to encourage flowering, cutting back all growth to within 2-3 buds of the base of the previous year's growth. Propagate by layering.

**VARIETIES** *W. sinensis (above)*, mauve or deep lilac flowers in 30cm/12in racemes; *W. floribunda*, to 10m/30ft, violet flowers in 20cm/8in racemes; *W. f. alba*, white, with 60cm/24in racemes; *W. f. violacea plena*, violet double flowers; *W. f. macrobotrys*, blue racemes may reach over 90cm/3ft long.

**POSSIBLE PROBLEMS** Birds may damage buds and flowers; aphids; bud-drop if soil dries out or after overnight frost.

## ▮ PROPAGATION TIP

*The fruits that appear on* passiflora *contain seeds that can be sown in spring or when ripe, but the quality of plants obtained in this way cannot be guaranteed. A more reliable way of propagating a really good performer is to take semi-ripe cuttings in summer, with base heat to speed up rooting.*

## ▮ PLANTING TIP

Wisteria *can easily be grown from seed, but they may take several years to start flowering and the quality of flower is by no means assured. In the right situation, they grow to a great age and size, so it is worth starting with a good specimen. To avoid disappointment, look out for grafted plants instead.*

125

# GLOSSARY

**Acid** Used to describe soil with a pH reading below 7.0. Because acid soils contain little lime, lime-hating plants like rhododendrons thrive in them.

**Aeration** Loosening of the soil to admit air.

**Alkaline** Used to describe soil with a pH reading above 7.0. A slightly alkaline soil suits most plants.

**Annual** A plant that completes its life cycle in one growing season

**Aquatic** A plant that lives in water, sometime.with leaves and flowers floating on the surface.

**Axil** The angle between the stem and a leaf, from which further growth arises.

**Bedding plant** A plant used for temporary garden display.

**Biennial** A plant that needs two growing seasons to complete its life cycle.

**Bract** A modified leaf, which may he coloured and have the appearance of a petal.

**Bulbil** A small bulb that forms at the base of mature bulbs and which can be detached and grown on to achieve maturity.

**Chlorosis** Deficiency of minerals in the soil giving a pale appearance to foliage.

**Cloche** Glass or plastic covering to protect plants in the open.

**Compost 1** a mixture of loam, sand, peat and leaf-mould used for growing plants in containers.
        **2** rotted remains of plant and other organic material.

**Corona** From the Latin meaning a crown. Used to describe the trumpet of a narcissus.

**Crown** The bottom of a perennial such as lupin from which roots and shoots arise.

**Dead-heading** The practice of removing faded flowerheads in order to prevent seeding, encourage further flowering or to keep a plant looking tidy.

**Dormant** Literally, sleeping. Used to describe the period when a plant makes no growth usually in the winter.

**Evergreen** A plant which bears foliage throughout the year.

**Fungicide** A substance used to combat fungal diseases.

**Germination** The first stage in the development of a plant from a seed.

**Ground cover** Plants used to cover the soil smothering weeds with attractive foliage.

**Half-hardy** Used to describe plants that require protection during the winter.

**Hardy** Description of plants that survive frost in the open.

**Hip** Fruit of the rose.

**Humus** The substance remaining when dead vegetable matter has broken down.

**Insecticide** A substance used for killing insects.

**Larva** The immature stage of some insects, such as caterpillars and grubs.

**Lateral** A stem or shoot that branches out from the leaf axil of a larger stem.

**Leader** The main stem of a tree that extends the system of branches.

**Lime** Calcium, a chemical that may be used to neutralize acid soils. Too much lime makes it impossible for some nutrients in the soil to be absorbed by plants.

**Loam** Soil which is a compound of clay, silt, sand and humus. It is moisture-retentive and mineral-rich.

**Mulch** A layer of organic matter spread on the soil surface to conserve moisture.

**Naturalizing** The practice of growing plants in conditions that simulate nature.

**Neutral** Used to describe soil with a pH reading between 6.5 and 7.0, which is neither acid nor alkaline.

**Node** A joint in a plant's stem from which leaves, buds and side-shoots arise.

**Offset** A young plant that is naturally produced by mature plants and can be detached and used for propagation.

**Organic** Used to describe substances that are the product of the decay of living organisms.

**Peat** Partially decayed organic matter. Sedge peat is from the roots of sedges growing in bogs.

**Perennial** A plant that lives for an indefinite period.

**pH reading** The pH scale is used to measure the acidity or alkalinity of soil. The neutral point is 7.0; a reading above this denotes alkalinity and one below it denotes acidity.

**Pinching out** Removing the growing point of a stem to encourage bushy growth.

**Pricking out** Planting out seedlings for the first time to larger trays or to a nursery bed.

**Propagation** Increasing plants.

**Pruning** Cutting back a plant to keep the shape neat, restrict the size and encourage the formation of flowers.

**Root run** The soil area occupied by the roots of a plant.

**Rootstock** The name for the plant on to which another is grafted.

**Scion** A shoot of a plant joined to the rootstock of another. Used to propagate trees.

**Seedling** A young plant.

**Stake** A support for plants, from a cane for delphiniums to a heavy wooden stake for a young tree.

**Stamen** The male reproductive organ of a flower, arising from the centre of the petals.

**Sucker** A shoot that arises from below ground level. Suckers should always be pulled clean off, not cut.

**Tender** Used to describe any plant susceptible to damage by frost.

**Tendril** A kind of leaf or stem that twines around supports, permitting plants to climb.

**Tilth** The surface layer of the soil, which is fine and crumbly.

**Transplanting** Moving young plants from one place to another to give them more room to develop.

**Vegetative** Propagation by a part of the plant, i.e. offsets, cuttings, division of roots, layering of a stem, rather than by sowing seeds.

**Whorl** An arrangement of leaves or flowers that project from a single point like rays.

# INDEX